Sales Management Control, Territory Design, Sales Force Performance, and Sales Organizational Effectiveness in the Pharmaceutical Industry

Eric Longino

DISSERTATION.COM

Boca Raton

Sales Management Control, Territory Design, Sales Force Performance, and
Sales Organizational Effectiveness in the Pharmaceutical Industry

Dissertation.com
Boca Raton, Florida
USA • 2009

ISBN-10: 1-59942-706-0
ISBN-13: 978-1-59942-706-5

ABSTRACT

Limited research exists about the determinants of sales organization effectiveness in pharmaceutical sales organizations. To fill this void sales management control, sales territory design, and sales force performance are conceptualized as antecedents to sales organization effectiveness in pharmaceutical sales organizations. The results of the structural equation model tested suggested that pharmaceutical sales representatives perform better and are more effective when they are satisfied with sales territory design because of its significant relationship with sales force behavioral performance. The present study suggest sales force behavioral performance leads to sales organization effectiveness through its significant relationship to sales force outcome performance. These findings are somewhat different to those from similar studies in other industries, and identify some important implications for sales leaders in the pharmaceutical industry as well as suggesting a number of important research directions.

ACKNOWLEDGMENTS

The completion of a dissertation does not reflect all the effort of numerous individuals involved in the process. I express my gratitude and appreciation for the support and contribution of everyone who assisted me during this endeavor.

Specifically, I would like to offer my thanks to my committee chairperson, Dr. Elliot Ser for his encouragement and assistance in this journey. I appreciate his positive reinforcement and encouragement during challenging times in the process. I also thank the members of my dissertation committee, Dr. Craig Barton and Dr. Herbert M. Turner, III, for their valuable insights into the research and writing process. Particularly, I would like to thank Dr. Turner for his encouragement from start to finish.

I also express gratitude to my classmates at the University of Phoenix for their encouragement and support. I express gratitude to my supervisor Denice Torres for her support and encouragement throughout the process. In addition, I express gratitude to my academic counselor Misa Alexander for her support throughout the process. I also express appreciation to my employer for allowing me to conduct this study.

Finally, I express my deepest gratitude to my family for their support in completing this goal. I thank my parents Aaron and Mary Longino for their unconditional love and support. I also thank my sister and brother, Aaron Longino, Jr., and Denice Boone for their encouragement and support throughout the process. I also thank my children, Evan-Eric, Mykal-Michele and Jordan Andrew, for their support despite the many hours devoted to this endeavor. Lastly, I especially thank my wife, Tayna, for her support, devotion, and encouragement in fulfilling this aspiration.

TABLE OF CONTENTS

LIST OF TABLES.. xi

LIST OF FIGURES xii

CHAPTER 1: INTRODUCTION 1

Background of the Problem 4

Statement of the Problem... 9

Purpose of the Study 10

Significance of the Study... 11

Significance of the Study to Leadership 12

Nature of the Study 15

Research Question 16

Hypotheses... 17

Theoretical Framework 18

      Agency Theory 19

      Organization Theory 20

      Transaction Cost Analysis 21

Definition of Terms... 22

Assumptions.. 23

Limitations 23

Delimitations... 24

Summary 25

CHAPTER 2: REVIEW OF THE LITERATURE 28

Documentation... 31

Literature Gap within Pharmaceuticals Sales 32

Sales Management Control Journal Research.. 33

Dissertation Research on Sales Management Control 33

Salesperson Performance Research 35

      The Walker Expectancy Motivation Framework 36

      Expectancy Framework Research.. 37

      The Weitz Contingency Perspective.. 39

      Contingency Framework Research... 41

      Sales Behaviors.. 42

Management Control 44

Theories of Sales Management Control... 47

Systems of Sales Management Control 49

      Research about Control Systems for Sales Management 51

      Sales Management Control Research in the Pharmaceutical Industry 64

Sales Territory Design 66

Sales Force Performance.. 69

Sales Organization Effectiveness... 72

Conclusion 74

Summary... 76

CHAPTER 3: METHOD 80

Research Design... 80

Appropriateness of Design... 82

Research Question 82

Hypotheses 83

Population 83

Sampling Frame 85

Sample Size 87

Informed Consent 88

Confidentiality 88

Geographic Location 89

Data Collection 89

Instrumentation 89

     Reliability 92

Validity: Internal and External 93

     Internal Validity 95

     External Validity 95

     Content and Construct Validity 95

Data Analysis 96

Summary 100

CHAPTER 4: RESULTS 103

Data Analysis Process 103

Stage 1: Pre-Analysis Data Examination and Data Preparation 103

     Population and Sample Selection 103

     Descriptive Statistics for the Individual Items 104

     Missing Values 112

     Missing Value Analysis 113

Univariate Outliers.. 114

Stage 2: Validation of the Measures 116

    Assessing Reliability and Validity of Constructs and Indicators 118

Stage 3: Correlation Analysis of Constructs and Hypotheses 123

    Null Hypothesis 1 124

    Null Hypothesis 2 124

    Null Hypothesis 3 125

    Null Hypothesis 4 126

    Null Hypothesis 5 127

    Null Hypothesis 6 127

    Null Hypothesis 7 127

Stage 4: Assessing the Structural Model and Path Estimates.......................... 128

    Structural Equation Model Analysis.. 128

Summary 135

CHAPTER 5: CONCLUSIONS AND RECOMMENDATIONS.................... 138

Conclusions.. 139

    Pre-analysis Data Examination and Data Preparation 140

    Validation of the Measures.. 140

    Hypothesis One... 141

    Hypothesis Two... 142

    Hypothesis Three.. 142

    Hypothesis Four.. 143

    Hypothesis Five 144

Hypothesis Six 144

Hypothesis Seven 145

Structural Equation Model 145

Implications of the Findings 148

Implications for Pharmaceutical Sales Force Leadership 151

Recommendation for Action by Stakeholders 153

Recommendations for Future Research 154

Summary 157

REFERENCES 160

APPENDIX A: COMMUNICATION WITH SUBJECTS 180

APPENDIX B: INFORMED CONSENT 181

APPENDIX C: RESEARCH QUESTIONNAIRE 183

APPENDIX D: BOXPLOTS 187

APPENDIX E: MODIFICATION INDICES 195

APPENDIX F: MODEL STANDARDIZED PARAMETER ESTIMATES ... 201

APPENDIX G: AMOS FINAL OUTPUT 202

APPENDIX H: VERBAL SCRIPT 217

APPENDIX I: RESEARCH HYPOTHESES 218

APPENDIX J: PERMISSION TO USE MATERIALS 220

LIST OF TABLES

Table 1. *ML Estimates of Structural Parameters and Model Statistic (Field Sales Manager Sample N = 146)[a]* 59

Table 2. *Correlations and Reliability Estimates (N = 146)* 94

Table 3. *Summary of Variables and Hypothesis Analysis* 97

Table 4. *Participants' Profile* 105

Table 5. *Descriptive Statistics for Individual Items* 106

Table 6. *Variable Transformation* 115

Table 7. *Composite Reliability and Variance Extracted Estimates* 119

Table 8. *Correlations, Means and Standard Deviations (N = 151)* 125

Table 9. *Measurement Model Parameter Estimates (N = 151)* 132

Table 10. *Structural Coefficients in Metric Form (N = 151)* 133

Table 11. *Structural Coefficients in Standard Form (N = 151)* 134

Table 12. *Effects of Independents on Sales Organization Effectiveness* 135

LIST OF FIGURES

Figure 1. Sales organization design framework. 57

Figure 2. Empirical model used for the proposed study 81

Figure 3. Basic model of sales organization effectiveness ($N = 151$). 117

Figure 4. Model of sales organization effectiveness with standardized parameter estimates ($N = 151$). 148

CHAPTER 1: INTRODUCTION

Many firms employ complex selling organizations to interact with consumers.

Large companies rely on an internal sales force composed of many hierarchical positions,

such as a regional manager, district manager, and territory sales representative; outsource

selling to independent selling organizations and their sales forces; or employ a

combination of the two to connect products and/or services to customers. According to

the Bureau of Labor Statistics (1997), sales and marketing in 1996 accounted for close to

14.5 million jobs in the United States. The number of sales and marketing jobs is

predicted to increase by 15.5% to 16.8 million jobs by 2006.

According to Corcoran, Peterson, Baitch, and Barrett (1996), when identifying

factors affecting sales organization performance, the sales job warrants rigorous

examination. Long-term growth and profitability for sales organizations are dependent on

the effectiveness of their salespeople. Therefore, salesperson effectiveness is a key

success factor for sales organizations. The salesperson's role is to translate company

strategy from goal to actual sales and is expected to add value for customers by creating

competitive product differentiation and contributing to a company's profitability.

A survey of 200 corporate executives conducted as part of the 2002/2003

Accenture High Performance Workforce Study illustrated how critical the sales force is to

corporate success (Accenture, 2003a). The 200 corporate executives surveyed identified

sales as the most important corporate function. In addition, most executives who viewed

sales as an important function also thought their sales force could achieve higher

performance. Results from the 2003 *Selling in Turbulent Times Survey* conducted by

Accenture (2003b) and the Economist Intelligence Unit suggested global executives

1

believe their sales forces are ineffective. In a poll of 178 global executives, 56% believed their sales forces' performance was mediocre, 26% thought their sale force performance was below average, and 2% described their sales forces' performance as disappointing.

According to Corcoran et al. (1996), generating sales leads is an important function of the sales job. Only 38% of the executives in the *Selling in Turbulent Times Survey* (Accenture, 2003b) thought salespeople were not generating enough leads. The ability to manage sales opportunities appeared to be a greater problem than not having enough leads, which suggested that the root cause of mediocre sales performance is not the economic environment but shortcomings in the behaviors and capabilities of the salespeople themselves. Due to increasing competition, sales have become difficult to obtain. The increasing competition has exposed weaknesses in corporate selling, namely, critical performance issues, previously concealed or minimized by a growth market, that threaten to limit sales force effectiveness.

The results of the *Accenture High Performance Workforce Study* (Accenture, 2003a) and *Selling in Turbulent Times Survey* (Accenture, 2003b) indicated that many corporate executives' belief is that the performance of most economic companies is heavily dependent on the sales force. As a result, companies closely monitor the performance and profitability of their sales forces. According to Zoltners and Lorimer (2000), sales forces cost American companies over $500 billion a year. Heide (1999) reported the cost of a sales call in many industries is over $200. Sales forces are a major investment for many companies, with the largest sales forces costing billions of dollars a year to deploy and support.

The high cost of a sales force requires sales organizations to maximize sales performance. According to Zoltners and Lorimer (2000), sales managers feel the pressure to improve sales force performance with fewer resources. Numerous books and articles discuss how trends like benchmarking (Smith, Ritter, & Tuggle, 1995), reengineering (Blessington & O'Connell, 1995), total quality management (Cortada, 1993), and downsizing (Lucus, 1996) can be applied to the sales force. Companies have hired and continue to hire consultants, establish taskforces, and set up departments to deal with sales force performance issues (Zoltners & Lorimer, 2000).

Past research (Churchill, Ford, Hartley, & Walker, 1985; Mount & Barrick, 1995; Vinchur, Schippmann, Switzer, & Roth, 1998) attempted to understand and/or improve sales force performance by examining the characteristics of individual salesperson performance. These studies have not adequately explained the variation in sales force performance. A small but growing body of research has focused on the importance of situational contingencies such as systems of sales management control and territory design choices (Grant & Cravens, 1996). These emerging studies suggested that situational contingencies such as control systems for sales management may act as moderators and/or predictors of sales force performance in economic organizations (Babakus, Cravens, Grant, Ingram, & LaForge, 1996; Cravens, Ingram, LaForge, & Young, 1993; Darmon, 1993; Ganesan, Weitz, & John, 1993; Grant & Cravens, 1996; Oliver & Anderson, 1994; Piercy, Cravens, & Morgan, 1999; Weitz, Sujan, & Sujan, 1986). The emerging body of research is focused on sales management and sales organization practices, rather than the characteristics of individual salespeople. The present study contributes to this emerging body of research by examining how certain dimensions of sales management and sales organization practices influence sales force performance in sales organizations within the pharmaceutical industry.

Background of the Problem

Trends in pharmaceutical sales generation show the influence of competition, pricing, and cost pressures on company revenue growth (Seget, 2004). Four main resistors to pharmaceutical sales growth have resulted in pressure on the sales force to deliver improved performance:

1. Cost containment in major healthcare markets

2. Competition from generic companies and parallel importers

3. High research and development costs and falling productivity

4. Merger and acquisition investments.

Rising cost containment measures have resulted from the increased demands on national healthcare payers and providers brought about by an aging population and the subsequent increase in those suffering from acute and chronic conditions (Seget, 2004). A range of cost containment policies is used across different national markets, including pricing regulations, strict reimbursement formularies, and a growth in both generic substitution and parallel importing. These measures lead to increased pressure on pharmaceutical companies to reduce their prices and, consequently, either increase unit sales or reduce costs to maintain profit margins. Maximizing return on investment from sales and promotional activities is a key factor for both increasing unit sales and limiting the cost base.

Generic substitution and parallel imports have become central policies in the drive for healthcare cost containment (Seget, 2004). National reimbursement and insurance

4

bodies have increasingly provided physicians and pharmacists with incentives for prescribing cheaper generic drugs. Products with an estimated $100 billion worth of revenues will have lost patent protection between 2001 and 2005. As a result, pharmaceutical companies face growing competition from generic companies, which negatively influences revenues before and after product patent expiry. Seget suggested pharmaceutical companies would need to maximize sales force effectiveness and allocate promotional budgets appropriately to maintain market share.

Research and development expenditures have increased over the last 20 years of the 20th century, both in absolute terms and relative to sales growth. According to Seget (2004), absolute research and development expenditures increased from approximately $2 million to $30 million between 1980 and 2003, representing a compound annual growth rate of 13.1%. Research and development, as a proportion of total sales, has also shown an upward trend since 1980, increasing from 9% to 16% in 2003.

According to Sahoo (2005), legal and regulatory responses to drug safety issues will increase drug research and development costs. Since the withdrawal of Vioxx in September 2004, legal and regulatory responses to drug safety issues have accelerated. Lawmakers and regulators seek to evaluate and change the drug research and development process to minimize drug safety risks. As a result, the Food and Drug Administration (FDA) is more closely scrutinizing the drug approval process, which can delay drug approval. For drugs with revenues of $1 billion or more each year, for every day drug approval is delayed in the FDA approval process, it costs its developer an estimated $1.3 million.

In addition, the FDA requires additional post-marketing studies, also called phase IV studies (Sahoo, 2005). Phase IV studies are clinical trials required by the FDA to be completed by a pharmaceutical company. Such studies are initiated after the FDA has approved a product for sale. Phase IV studies provide additional information about a product's safety, efficacy, and optimal use. Although Phase IV investigations were relatively rare in the 1980s and early 1990s, their use has been growing as safety issues become more common. To reduce safety risks, FDA regulations have been updated to address and formalize the use of post-marketing studies. The results of these regulatory actions are increased research and development costs and declining margin growth. Therefore, current drugs in development are subject to pressure to achieve high sales in order for profitability to be maintained.

As research and development costs increase, research and development productivity levels diminish. The number of drugs approved by the FDA has fluctuated, resulting in a decline in overall productivity levels over the period 1994-2003 (Seget, 2004). The research and development costs for new drug approval increased from $611 million in 1994 to $949 million in 2003, equivalent to a compound annual growth rate of 5.0%. Because research and development productivity levels fall and costs increase, additional pressure is put on the sales and marketing function of companies to generate improved sales from each approved product in order to make up for the shortfall in drug approvals.

In the pharmaceutical industry, mergers and acquisitions are used for delivering critical mass in sales and research and development because these deals promise to deliver improved productivity and return on investment (Seget, 2004). While profit growth because of mergers and acquisition deals is limited, the industry's pursuit of mergers and acquisitions remains a priority. Deals between Pfizer and Pharmacia and Sanofi-Synthelabo and Aventis are examples of this trend. According to Seget, the merger of two pharmaceutical companies can provide several benefits. These benefits include increased market share, an improved product portfolio, and a broader geographic coverage. While these benefits are important, a primary critical success factor when two pharmaceutical companies merge is the successful integration of both companies' sales forces. According to Seget, merging two sales forces can be a complex and costly process. Another merger complication for pharmaceutical companies is the need to divest competing products. Divesting these products can result in lower market share and increased market and product competition.

While sales revenue growth has been under pressure from cost-containment measures, generic competition, rising research and development costs, and merger and acquisition investments, a pharmaceutical company's commercial expenses have also increased, both in absolute terms and as a proportion of total sales (Seget, 2004). Between 2000 and 2003, expenses for direct-to-consumer advertising, samples, sales force physician detailing, and journal advertising have increased. For example, the total promotional expenses of U.S. pharmaceutical companies increased to $25.3 billion in 2003, equivalent to a compound annual growth rate of 17.2% during the period 2000-2003. As a proportion of sales revenues, promotional expenses increased from 9.7% in 2000 to 11.9% in 2003.

Seget (2004) suggested that sales force physician detailing, including sampling, represents approximately 75% of total pharmaceutical sales and marketing expenditure and continues to be a key activity used to increase sales growth. However, the return on investment from sales force physician detailing is decreasing because of three key trends. First, across the industry, the number of pharmaceutical sales representatives has increased, thus increasing the level of competition between sales representatives to gain physician-detailing appointments. Second, sales representatives are increasingly targeting the same high prescribing physicians, further increasing competition for physicians' time. Third, physicians are increasingly unable to participate in salesperson detailing visits because of pressure to improve healthcare service efficiency, leaving less time available for salesperson detailing visits.

Achieving economies of scale, committing resources to new product launches, and providing technological support to increase efficiency contribute to sales force costs (Pushkala, Wittman, & Rauseo, 2006). According to Pushkala et al., technology costs will increase as more companies invest in sales force automation systems to increase sales force efficiency and effectiveness. In an environment characterized by rising costs and decreasing productivity, pharmaceutical companies must monitor the return on investment made from increases in sales force costs.

Because of the changing dynamics of the pharmaceutical industry and the changing needs of physicians, increasing sales force performance could become a key driver of success in the pharmaceutical industry. However, limited empirical research is available for improving sales force performance within the pharmaceutical industry. The present study is an attempt to fill this void by examining the influence of sales management and sales organization practices on sales force performance in sales organizations within the pharmaceutical industry.

Statement of the Problem

Pharmaceutical sales organizations' return on investment has decreased due to increased promotional expenses and lower revenue growth. As a proportion of sales revenues, promotional expenses increased from 9.7% in 2000 to 11.9% in 2003 (Seget, 2004). According to Seget, a primary factor of sales organization performance, namely, sales force physician detailing, represents 75% of total pharmaceutical sales organization promotional expenditure. Sales force physician detailing entails salespersons selling and providing samples of products to physicians.

According to Seget (2004), increased competition among salespeople and decreased detailing time with physicians has reduced sales force performance in pharmaceutical sales organizations. Limited research exists about what factors influence sales force performance in pharmaceutical sales organizations. Consequently, sales managers within pharmaceutical sales organizations lack information to improve sales force performance. Past research from other industries (Churchill et al., 1985; Mount & Barrick, 1995; Vinchur et al., 1998) attempted to help identify reliable and valid predictors of sales force performance. However, the hypothesized predictors explained little of the variation in sales force performance.

In the present quantitative study, an explanatory correlation research design is focused on the relationships between sales management control, sales territory design, sales force performance, and sales organization effectiveness and is used to provide pharmaceutical sales managers with information to improve sales force performance. The study population included first-line sales managers in the pharmaceutical industry.

According to Curry and Frost (2001), first-line sales managers are responsible for improving sales force performance in pharmaceutical sales organizations.

Purpose of the Study

The purpose of the present quantitative study is to use an explanatory correlation research design to examine the relationships between sales management control, sales territory design, sales force performance, and sales organization effectiveness in sales organizations within the pharmaceutical industry. The objective is to explain the magnitude of the relationships between the independent and dependent variables.

In a quantitative research methodology, problems in which trends need to be described or explanations developed for relationships between variables are studied (Creswell, 2002). In correlation research designs, a correlation technique is used to describe and measure the degree of association or relationship between two or more variables or sets of scores. Based on Creswell's description of a quantitative research methodology and correlation research design employing a quantitative research methodology, an explanatory correlation research design is appropriate. The target population is first-line sales managers within sales organizations in the pharmaceutical industry. The sample of sales managers was obtained from sales organizations within a pharmaceutical company located in the northeastern part of the United States.

The independent variables are sales management control, sales territory design, and sales force performance. The dependent variable is sales organization effectiveness. To maintain confidentiality, the pharmaceutical company providing the target population and sample was given the fictitious name of Octagon Pharmaceutical.

Significance of the Study

The results may offer insights about the predictors of improved sales force performance to sales management in sales organizations within the pharmaceutical industry. Determining what leads to superior sales force performance is an important aspect of every sales manager's job and may be critical to the survival and success of a firm (Muczyk & Gable, 1987). Considering that in 1996 sales and marketing accounted for close to 14.5 million jobs in the United States and sales and marketing jobs are predicted to increase by 15.5% to 16.8 million jobs by the year 2006 (Bureau of Labor Statistics, 1997), examining variables to improve sales force performance may benefit sales organizations within the pharmaceutical industry.

Pharmaceutical companies' sales revenue growth has declined due to increased competition, healthcare cost containment measures, and increased promotional expenses (Seget, 2004). Consequently, pharmaceutical companies must improve sales force performance to maximize return on investment. Limited empirical research exists about the factors that improve sales force performance in pharmaceutical sales organizations. According to Skelton (2004), the lack of empirical research about predictors for the performance of sales forces in the pharmaceutical industry is unexpected because the pharmaceutical industry has traditionally relied on its salespeople to establish and maintain profitable relationships with physicians and other healthcare customers. The lack of empirical research underscores the importance of understanding the predictors for sales force performance within sales organizations in the pharmaceutical industry.

Significance of the Study to Leadership

Leaders of pharmaceutical sales organizations may benefit from the present study in so much as the result may lead to an understanding of the relationships among certain dimensions of sales management and sales organization and the effect that those relationships have on sales performance. As a result, leaders of pharmaceutical sales organizations can proactively develop appropriate systems of sales management control to improve sales force performance. According to Grant and Cravens (1996), despite operating in a changing and competitive business environment, organizations are under pressure to increase shareholder value and returns. Consequently, the need to increase shareholder value and returns requires sales leaders to recognize the factors that improve sales performance within their organizations. In the pharmaceutical industry, where the selling environment has become increasingly competitive and regulatory pressures have had a negative influence on sales revenues, employing the appropriate systems of sales management control to improve sales force performance is essential (Seget, 2004).

The decline in sales revenue growth within the pharmaceutical industry originates from cost-containment measures, generic competition, rising research and development costs, and merger and acquisition investments (Seget, 2004). In addition, pharmaceutical companies' commercial expenses have increased, both in absolute terms and as a proportion of total sales. Due to the current competitive environment in the pharmaceutical industry, improving sales organization effectiveness is critical for current and future success (Skelton, 2004). However, because of limited empirical research about the predictors of sales organization effectiveness in the pharmaceutical industry, sales leaders in the industry have to depend on experience and unproven practices when determining resource allocation decisions.

According to Dubinsky, Yammarino, Jolson, and Spangler (1995), sales managers can have a dramatic influence on salespeople. Depending upon the leadership approach sales managers adopt, as well as other dimensions of the relationship between the manager and salesperson, sales managers can have positive, neutral, or negative effects on the salesperson's job satisfaction, motivation, and performance (Walker, Churchill, & Ford, 1979). A key to effective sales leadership and organizational effectiveness could be the establishment of an effective structure of sales personnel governance (Oliver & Anderson, 1994). Oliver and Anderson defined such a control system as an organization's set of procedures for manager supervision, guidance, assessment, and compensation of employees.

Oliver and Anderson (1994) proposed that two extreme points along a continuum characterize control systems. The two points provide two alternative management strategies labeled outcome-based and behavior-based control. An *outcome-based control system* involves relatively minimal management involvement with salespeople, reliance on objective sales results, and an increased compensation risk for the salesperson. An extensive level of supervisor monitoring, directing, and intervening in salespersons' activities typifies behavior-based control systems.

Methods used to evaluate behavior-based performance are subjective and more complex and typically centered on the salesperson's job inputs, like personal qualities, activities, and sales strategies (Oliver & Anderson, 1994). According to Oliver and Anderson, job inputs are not themselves indicators of results. Job inputs are salesperson

13

activities that are expected to generate future results. Compensation methods used for behavior-based control reduce the risk to the salesperson.

Oliver and Anderson (1994) argued that outcome-based and behavior-based control systems are opposite sales force strategies. Sales management may elect to position its sales force strategy at various levels between these extremes. Research (Babakus et al., 1996; Cravens et al., 1993; Oliver & Anderson, 1994) has suggested that the position management selects for a salesperson along the behavior-outcome continuum has numerous managerial consequences in terms of the salesperson's affect, cognition, behavior, and performance. Past research suggested a positive relationship between salesperson performance and sales organizational effectiveness (Babakus et al., 1996; Cravens et al., 1993; Churchill, Ford, & Walker, 1997). Improving the understanding of leaders in sales organizations about where to position its systems of sales management control could improve sales organization effectiveness.

Contemporary knowledge about sales management control indicated important inconsistencies in the conceptualization of control and its consequences (Baldauf, Cravens, & Piercy, 2005). According to Baldauf et al., research studies examining the antecedents and consequences of sales management control need to be organized. In addition, limited empirical research has been conducted on the effect of various sales force management control systems within sales organizations in the pharmaceutical industry. The present study could enhance sales organization leaders' understandings of the influence of control systems for sales management in sales organizations within the pharmaceutical industry.

Nature of the Study

The present quantitative study is an attempt to extend previous research about sales management control (Babakus et al., 1996; Piercy et al., 1999). Consistent with previous research about sales management control, an explanatory correlation research design was employed. Various authors refer to explanatory correlation research as "relational" research (Cohen & Manion, 1994, p. 123) or "explanatory" research (Fraenkel & Wallen, 2000, p. 360). The objective of correlation research is to explain the association between or among variables (Creswell, 2002).

The present study involved a pharmaceutical company located in the northeastern part of the United States. Hypotheses tested in previous research (Babakus et al., 1996; Piercy et al., 1999) with respect to the relationships between sales management control, sales territory design, sales force performance, and sales organizational effectiveness was tested by employing an explanatory correlation research design. Data was collected from first-line field sales managers, called district managers. A field sales unit, comprising a group of salespeople reporting to district managers, served as the unit of analysis. Consistent with previous research, which examined sales management control constructs (Babakus et al., 1996; Piercy et al., 1999), the district manager was selected as the appropriate information source for the study unit of analysis because the conceptual model tested for the present study incorporates organizational variables not easily evaluated by salespeople (Baldauf et al., 2000). According to Curry and Frost (2001), the majority of pharmaceutical sales organizations include salespeople reporting to district managers in the organizational structure. The sample included high performing, average performing, and low performing district managers as indicated by their annual sales performance ranking.

A variety of sales organizations with similar organizational structures within a single pharmaceutical company constituted the sample. In past research about sales management control, data was collected from salespersons within multiple selling environments (Cravens et al., 1993; Oliver & Anderson, 1994; Piercy, Cravens, & Morgan, 1998) or from sales managers employed by a diverse set of independently owned and operated sales agencies (Babakus et al., 1996). A limited number of the salespersons or sales managers sampled in previous studies that examined constructs associated with sales management control were from sales organizations in the pharmaceutical industry. The present study is an attempt to extend existing research about sales management control by examining these relationships in sales organizations within the pharmaceutical industry.

Research Question

Creswell (2002) defined research as a cyclical process of steps that typically begins with identifying a research problem or issue. Research involves reviewing the literature, specifying a purpose for the study, collecting and analyzing data, and formulating an interpretation of the information. The purpose of the process is to test hypotheses, analyze data, and add new knowledge to the field. The present study is focused on collecting and interpreting data to answer the following research question:

R1: What relationships exist between sales management control, sales territory design, sales force performance, and sales organization effectiveness in the pharmaceutical industry?

Examining these constructs in sales organizations within the pharmaceutical industry will extend and build on findings of past research about sales management control and distinguish between behavior-based and outcome-based sales management control approaches (Anderson & Oliver, 1987; Oliver & Anderson, 1994).

Hypotheses

Hypotheses are predictions about results when comparing groups or relating variables in a sample (Creswell, 2002). According to Creswell, the traditional form of writing hypotheses is to state them as null hypotheses. Null hypotheses predict that no relationships or differences exist among variables or groups for measured variables in the general population. The present study evaluated the following null hypotheses:

$H1_0$: No significant correlation exists between the level of sales force behavioral performance and the level of sales force outcome performance.

$H2_0$: No significant correlation exists between the level of sales force outcome performance and the level of sales organization effectiveness.

$H3_0$: No significant correlation exists between the extent of behavior-based sales management control and the level of sales force behavioral performance.

$H4_0$: No significant correlation exists between the extent of behavior-based sales management control and the level of satisfaction with sales territory design.

$H5_0$: No significant correlation exists between the extent of satisfaction with sales territory design and the level of sales organization effectiveness.

$H6_0$: No significant correlation exists between the extent of satisfaction with sales territory design and the level of sales force behavioral performance.

$H7_0$: No significant correlation exists between the extent of satisfaction with sales

territory design and the level of sales force outcome performance.

Consistent with prior research about management control in other industries (Babakus et al., 1996; Cravens et al., 1993; Piercy et al., 1999), the hypotheses tested were used to answer the research question.

Theoretical Framework

The theoretical framework is based on a sales management control system. According to Anderson and Oliver (1987), a *control system* is an organization's set of procedures for manager supervision, guidance, assessment, and compensation of its employees. Anderson and Oliver conceptualized two different philosophies of sales management control: behavior-based control and outcome-based control. A behavior-based control system emphasizes the use of field sales managers, coupled with an emphasis on fixed-salary compensation to direct and control the behaviors of salespeople. An outcome-based control system, in contrast, replaces behavior control of field sales managers and fixed compensation with a focus on controlling sales force outcomes using incentive compensation.

Theories relevant to sales force control is agency theory, organization theory, and transaction cost analysis (Anderson & Oliver, 1987; Stathakopoulos, 1996). Each theory addresses sales force control using different assumptions and identifies different sets of variables (Anderson & Oliver, 1987). According to Stathakopoulos (1996), theoretical approaches can assist managers with determining the circumstances under which a behavior-based control system or outcome-based control system should be employed.

Agency Theory

Agency theory is a normative microeconomics or accounting approach for finding optimal and profit-maximizing forms of control (Bergen, Dutta, & Walker, 1992; Eisenhardt, 1985). The theory includes the principal, the agent, environmental uncertainty, and the realized results. An agency relationship exists whenever one party, the principal, delegates to another party, the agent, a service to be performed for compensation. The principal attempts to control the activities of agents in order to maximize the principal's utility. The central premise of the theory is that principals and agents have divergent goals. For example, a sales manager, the principal, might want the sales force, the agents, to spend more time servicing current accounts, but the salesperson might prefer to spend more time finding new accounts.

In agency theory, sales force control can be based on either behavior or outcomes (Anderson & Oliver, 1987). When factors to improve sales force performance are known, a principal can specify desired agent behavior in order to maximize the principal's utility. When factors to improve sales force performance are unknown, principals base agent control on observable behavior; however, an agent's behavior is assumed to be unobservable under conditions of high uncertainty or low-task programmability. *Task programmability* is the degree to which sales managers can specify clearly the selling and nonselling activities a salesperson must perform to achieve a desired outcome (Eisenhardt, 1985; Ouchi, 1977). Under conditions of incomplete information, the agent is aware of his or her behavior, but the principal is not; agency models address the risk-bearing preferences of the principal and the agent (Eisenhardt, 1985). Risk bearing relates to the risk in the environment due to environmental uncertainty.

19

Organization Theory

The premise of organization theory is to link task characteristics and control systems (Eisenhardt, 1985; Ouchi 1979). Consistent with the normative model, two environmental factors, namely task programmability and outcome observables, require assessment to determine a control system (Eisenhardt, 1985). According to Eisenhardt, if a task's programmability is known, the behaviors needed for its successful performance can be realized, thus supporting a sales manager's use of behavior controls. If task programmability is high but outcome observables are low, behavior control is the only feasible choice.

Eisenhardt (1985) linked task programmability with knowledge of the transformation process, or the process through which employee behaviors generate system outcomes. According to Eisenhardt, if knowledge of the process is high, appropriate behavior can be defined explicitly and selling and nonselling activities can be standardized a priori. As such knowledge decreases, behavior-based control becomes difficult to use because effective behavior cannot be specified and no basis exists for monitoring the appropriateness of salesperson behavior in relation to intentions (Eisenhardt, 1985; Ouchi, 1977). For example, salespersons may have developed clear scripts for sales performance (Leigh & McGraw, 1989; Weitz et al., 1986) and may be able to articulate these action scripts to new salespersons. In contrast, a sales manager may know a salesperson's call rate, but may not know whether the optimal strategy is to call at the same rate, make more calls on more customers, make more calls on fewer customers, or make fewer calls (Anderson & Oliver, 1987).

Transaction Cost Analysis

Transaction cost analysis is an appropriate framework for examining control mechanisms (Williamson, 1985). In the sales force context, the transaction cost is the cost of performing, monitoring, and controlling the activities of the sales force (John & Weitz, 1989). According to transaction cost analysis, outcome-based control mechanisms are preferable. Outcome-based controls are cost efficient when the market is highly competitive because outcome-based controls correspond to market contracting when the firm contracts the salespeople to make sales. The salespeople are monitored only on the basis of sales generated because sales made are considered the market signals of how successful and efficient salespeople are.

In terms of transaction cost analysis, the circumstances under which behavior-based control is appropriate are recognized. One such situation occurs when a salesperson has transaction-specific assets; these are specialized assets or experiences of high value to the firm (John & Weitz, 1989). For example, the salesperson may have acquired valuable knowledge of special procedures and policies for placing orders, servicing customers, and servicing key accounts. Such a salesperson may be difficult to replace because the firm would have to incur training costs to develop such skills in newly hired salespeople. Experienced salespeople are thought to practice opportunistic sales behavior without fear of reprimand. According to John and Weitz, retaining such salespeople under these circumstances, while discouraging opportunistic behavior and maintaining firm loyalty, requires firms to shift toward behavior-based control.

Definition of Terms

Systems of sales management control: An organization has a set of procedures for supervising, guiding, assessing, and compensating its employees (Anderson & Oliver, 1987). According to Anderson and Oliver, systems of sales management control can be classified as those evaluating the outcome of a process and those assessing individual stages in the process, outcome-based and behavior-based systems respectively.

Sales territory design: Sales territory design encompasses such issues as determining the size of the sales force and territory, determining territory boundaries, assigning customer account responsibility, and deploying a salesperson's selling time across customers and prospects (Piercy et al., 1999).

Sales force performance: Researchers divide sales force performance into two separate dimensions: the behavior or activities performed by salespeople and the outcomes or results attained by their efforts. The two dimensions are labeled as behavior-based performance and outcome-based performance (Anderson & Oliver, 1987; Behrman & Perreault, 1982).

Behavior-based performance: According to Piercy et al. (1999), behavior-based performance is concerned with the various work activities, skills, and competencies needed to perform the responsibilities of the sales job. Job behaviors may include sales calls scheduling, sales calls planning, adaptive selling, and customer support activities.

Outcome-based performance: Outcome-based performance consists of the results attributable to the salesperson (Piercy et al., 1999). According to Piercy et al., traditional measures of salesperson outcome-based performance include territory market share, sales volume, and number of new accounts.

Sales organization effectiveness: Churchill et al. (1985) defined sales organization effectiveness as a summary evaluation of overall organizational outcomes. These organizational outcomes may refer to the entire sales organization or an organizational subset such as a region, district, territory, or customer group.

Assumptions

A primary assumption is that the findings are consistent with past findings that systems of sales management control play a critical role in (a) designing effective field sales organizations and (b) influencing behavior- and outcome-based performance (Babakus et al., 1996; Cravens et al., 1993; Grant & Cravens, 1996; Piercy et al., 1999). Additional assumptions included that participating sales managers will answer the questions on the administered questionnaire honestly, the information gathered from the participants will be reliable and valid, and the results will accurately reflect relationships between the independent variables and the dependent variable.

Limitations

The scope of the present study was limited to district managers in a sales organization within the pharmaceutical industry. The influence of sales management control, sales territory design, sales force performance, and sales organization effectiveness in a sales organization within the pharmaceutical industry was examined. The data collection activities associated with the present study was limited to Octagon Pharmaceutical. The study was limited to district managers within Octagon Pharmaceutical and to the number of district managers surveyed and the amount of time and resources available to conduct the study. In addition, the reliability of the results was constrained by the reliability of the administered questionnaire.

A measurement of the construct of sales territory design will not consider all aspects of territory and field sales unit design. The multi-item scale does not directly account for factors such as product and/or market specialization, major account and team-selling sales approaches, and vertical organizational structure (Babakus et al., 1996). One measure of satisfaction with sales territory design is not an objective determination of the appropriateness of sales organization design. In addition, measurement of the study constructs required district managers to assess their own activities and those of their field sales unit. According to Baldauf, Cravens, and Piercy (2000), when using self-reported information some upward bias might be inherent in such data.

The conceptual model employed is appropriate for sales organizations that employ behavior-based control because the design of the field sales unit is likely to be more important in behavior-based management control systems than outcome-based management control systems (Babakus et al, 2006). Results from past studies (Babakus et al., 1996; Cravens et al., 1993; Grant & Cravens, 1996; Piercy et al., 1999) in other industries based on the same conceptual model suggested behavior-based management systems are more effective than outcome-based management systems in sales organizations.

Delimitations

The present study was limited to surveying district sales managers in a sales organization within the pharmaceutical industry and was focused on examining the relationships between sales management control, sales territory design, sales force performance, and sales organization effectiveness in a sales organization within the pharmaceutical industry. The target population was district managers within Octagon

Pharmaceutical. As such, only district managers from operating companies within Octagon Pharmaceutical were included in the sample. The sample plan for the present study called for 100 district managers. According to Creswell (2002), approximately 30 participants are required to relate variables in a correlation study.

The sampling approach was simple random sampling. According to Creswell (2002), simple random sampling is the most rigorous form of sampling. The intent of simple random sampling is to choose a sample that will be representative of the population. The present study may be able to generalize the findings of the sample to the study population because it uses simple random sampling.

The present study is an attempt to extend previous research about sales management control (Babakus et al., 1996; Cravens et al., 1993; Grant & Cravens, 1996; Piercy et al., 1999) in a new sample population. Therefore, the instrument used to collect data was consistent with earlier research. The scores from the instrument and the scales used have been reported and validated in earlier studies and have demonstrated reliability. By extending previous research and targeting a large sample, the present quantitative explanatory correlation research study is an attempt to generalize the results for the district management population to sales organizations in the pharmaceutical industry.

Summary

Trends in pharmaceutical sales generation have revealed the influence of competition and cost pressures on the sustainability of double-digit growth rates (Seget, 2004). These trends highlight the importance of pharmaceutical sales forces and their relative efficiency and productivity in increasing sales. While sales revenue growth has been under pressure from cost-containment measures, generic competition, rising research and development costs, and merger and acquisition investments, pharmaceutical companies' commercial expenses have increased both in absolute terms and as a proportion of total sales. Because of the changing dynamics of the pharmaceutical industry and the changing needs of physicians, increasing sales force performance will become a key factor for success in the pharmaceutical industry.

Much of the past research about the sales management field has focused on understanding and improving sales force performance by assessing the characteristics of individual salespersons' performances (Churchill et al., 1985; Mount & Barrick, 1995; Vinchur et al., 1998). These studies have not clarified what influence overall sales force performance and effectiveness have on sales organizations. Consequently, a small but expanding body of research has focused on the importance of such situational contingencies as systems of sales management control and territory design choices as moderators and/or predictors of sales force performance and effectiveness in sales organizations (Babakus et al., 1996; Cravens et al., 1993; Darmon, 1993; Ganesan et al., 1993; Grant & Cravens, 1996; Oliver & Anderson, 1994; Weitz et al., 1986). The majority of past sales management control research has been conducted outside of the pharmaceutical industry's sales organizations. By considering the relationships between sales management control, sales territory design, sales force performance, and sales organization effectiveness in sales organizations within the pharmaceutical industry, leaders within pharmaceutical sales organizations can take account of additional information in their decisions on the design and implementation of sales force management control systems for sales personnel.

26

Chapter 1 provided the framework for the present study. Chapter 2 will present an overview of the previous research conducted on the nature of the relationships between sales management control, sales territory design, sales force performance, and sales organization effectiveness.

CHAPTER 2: REVIEW OF THE LITERATURE

The purpose of the present study is to examine relationships between sales management control, sales territory design, sales force performance, and sales organization effectiveness in sale organizations within the pharmaceutical industry. Awareness of the predictors of sales organization effectiveness is critical to the pharmaceutical industry in the context of increasing competition, pressures to control costs, and the rising costs of sales. Seget (2004) posited that while sales revenue growth has been under pressure from cost-containment measures, generic competition, rising research and development costs, and merger and acquisition investments, pharmaceutical companies' commercial expenses have increased, both in absolute terms and as a proportion of total sales. Seget noted that total promotional expenses of pharmaceutical companies in the U.S. increased as a proportion of sales revenues from 9.7% in 2000 to 11.9% in 2003.

Despite changing market dynamics, decreasing revenue growth, and rising commercial expenses, limited empirical data are available within the pharmaceutical industry about the predictors of sales organization performance and effectiveness. Past research about sales management (Churchill et al., 1985; Mount & Barrick, 1995; Vinchur et al., 1998) focused on understanding and improving sales organization performance and effectiveness by assessing the characteristics of individual salesperson's performance in other industries. These studies have not clarified the factors that influence sales organization performance and effectiveness.

Consequently, an expanding body of research has focused on the importance of situational contingencies such as systems of sales management control and territory design choices (Grant & Cravens, 1996). These studies suggested that such situational

contingencies may act as moderators and/or predictors of sales organization performance

in economic organizations (Babakus et al., 1996; Cravens et al., 1993; Darmon, 1993;

Ganesan et al., 1993; Grant & Cravens, 1996; Oliver & Anderson, 1994; Piercy et al.,

1999; Weitz et al., 1986). The analysis of such contingencies is apparent in research that

is focused on sales management practices and sales organizations, rather than the

characteristics of individual salespeople. The present study contributes to this emerging

body of research by examining how certain dimensions of sales management and sales

organization practices influence sales force performance and effectiveness in sales

organizations within the pharmaceutical industry.

The constructs evaluated are sales management control, sales territory design,

sales force performance, and sales organization effectiveness. The literature review

conducted highlighted several motives for the evaluation of these constructs in sales

organizations within the pharmaceutical industry. First, these constructs are found in

previous studies of sales management processes (Babakus et al., 1996; Cravens et al.,

1993; Piercy et al., 1999, Piercy, Low, & Cravens, 2004), and modeling the interrelations

between these constructs follows the general propositions formulated by Walker et al.

(1979). Second, examining these constructs in sales organizations within the

pharmaceutical industry will build upon the findings of past research about sales

management control that distinguish between behavior-based and outcome-based sales

management control approaches (Anderson & Oliver, 1987; Oliver & Anderson, 1994).

Cravens et al. (1993) identified field sales management control and compensation control as primary indicators of behavior-based and outcome-based control in sales organizations.

Third, previous sales management control research (Babakus et al., 1996; Oliver & Anderson, 1994; Piercy et al., 1999, Piercy et al., 2004) recognized the important distinction between the effectiveness of the sales organization and the performance of salespeople (Cravens et al., 1993; Walker et al., 1979). In addition, the sales performance construct is subdivided further into behavioral performance and outcome performance (Cravens et al., 1993). Behavioral performance, outcome performance, and sales organization effectiveness are considered separate constructs in this study because they are demonstrated to be conceptually distinct in past research (Babakus et al., 1996).

Fourth, the research literature included various studies of sales organization structure, sale force size, territory design, and the allocation of selling efforts (Beswick & Cravens, 1977; LaForge & Cravens, 1985; Lodish, 1980; Rangaswamy, Sinha, & Zoltners, 1990; Zoltners & Sinha, 1983; Zoltners, Sinha, & Zoltners, 2001). However, these studies focused on sales territory design in isolation from other sales management activities. The present study attempts to integrate the sales territory design variable into an overall sales organization effectiveness framework by recognizing that the antecedents of sales organization effectiveness include the management control system employed by the organization, the design of the territories assigned to salespeople, and sales force performance (Babakus et al., 1996; Piercy et al., 1999; Piercy et al., 2004). Exploring these relationships within sales organizations in the pharmaceutical industry in particular may provide information pharmaceutical sales managers could use to improve sales organization effectiveness.

In the literature review, previous research is examined, literature searches of databases are summarized, and the gap in the literature with respect to sales management control in the pharmaceutical industry is discussed and past sales performance research reviewed. In addition, management control research, underlying theories of control systems for sales management, and past research on the sales management control system constructs is explored. Past research on sales territory design, predictors of sales force performance and sales organization effectiveness are also examined.

Documentation

Several databases were explored to identify studies relevant to the research question and hypotheses posed. The University of Phoenix Library databases searched included EBSCOhost, ProQuest, Business Insights, Business Source Primer, Datamonitor Business Information Center, ProQuest Dissertations and Thesis, and Emerald. Other databases searched included Google Scholar, Questia Online Library, and UCLA Online Library.

The word search focused on the following terms: personal selling, personal sales management, sales management, sales performance, salesperson, selling skills, sales training, management control, sales management control, outcome-based control, behavior-based control, sales force control systems, sales force effectiveness, pharmaceutical sales, pharmaceutical sales force, biotech sales, biotech sales force, industrial sales force, retail sales force, sales territory, sales territory design, territory alignment, sales alignment, selling skills, selling behaviors, and adaptive selling. A comprehensive list of search terms resulted in a comprehensive and unbiased collection of the available literature.

Literature Gap within Pharmaceuticals Sales

Researchers have shown a high level of interest in the relationship between management control and sales and marketing effectiveness (Baldauf et al., 2005). The intent of management control in an organization is to direct and influence the attitudes and behaviors of employees to achieve organizational objectives (Anderson & Oliver, 1987; Eisenhardt, 1985; Jaworski, 1988, Ouchi, 1979). Sales management control considers the extent of sales manager activities such as supervising, guiding, assessing, and compensating salespeople (Anderson & Oliver, 1987).

Existing knowledge about marketing and sales management control is based on two seminal conceptual developments (Baldauf et al., 2005). First, Anderson and Oliver (1987), drawing from theoretical approaches in economics, organizational behavior, and psychology, conceptualized a formal management control framework and formulated propositions about the consequences of behavior-based and outcome-based sales force control (Baldauf et al., 2005). Second, Jaworski (1988) proposed a conceptualization consisting of formal and informal dimensions of management control for marketing personnel (Baldauf et al., 2005).

Based on the importance of understanding the predictors for sales organization effectiveness in the pharmaceutical industry, the literature review for the present study examined existing empirical research about the influence of behavior-based and outcome-based management control systems on sales force performance and sales organization effectiveness in sales organizations within the pharmaceutical industry. Included in the review are peer-reviewed journals, dissertation databases, and textbooks about the topic. The search rendered one empirical study that examined the effects of sales management control in sales organizations in the pharmaceutical industry. Considering the importance of the sales force to pharmaceutical companies' profitability, the lack of research on sales management control appears to be an oversight.

Sales Management Control Journal Research

Baldauf et al. (2005) synthesized various initiatives in research about sales management control in order to guide further research about the topic and found 22 articles that examined management control relationships. According to Baldauf et al., much of the empirical research was centered on sales organizations' examination of the management control relationships within the sales area and employment of sales executives (Babakus et al., 1996; Baldauf, et al., 2001; Cravens et al., 1993; Slater & Olsen, 2000), field sales management (Babakus et al., 1996; Baldauf et al., 2001; Piercy et al., 2004), and salespeople (Challagalla & Shervani, 1996; Krafft, 1999; Oliver & Anderson, 1994). The articles did not examine relationships of sales management control in sales organizations within the pharmaceutical industry.

Dissertation Research on Sales Management Control

Dissertations about topics related to the pharmaceutical industry (Allen, 2001; Ryerson, 2003; Saenz, 2004; Swanson, 2003; Thompson, 2002; Zhong, 2001) did not examine relationships of sales management control in sales organizations within the pharmaceutical industry. Saenz (2004) studied factors that influence physician drug prescribing in the pharmaceutical industry and found weak relationships for pharmaceutical representatives, direct to-consumer advertising, patient requests for specific medication, and physician prescribing. Ryerson (2003) used a sample of pharmaceutical representatives to study self-efficacy and sales performance and observed that self-efficacy could provide an explanation for sales performance. Zhong (2001) attempted to assess the relationship between a pharmaceutical sales representative's selling ability and sales performance and detected no positive relationships for adaptive selling beliefs, sensing or evaluating dimensions of listening skills, interactive presentation skills, and sales performance.

Several dissertations about sales management control were identified (Lopez, 2000; Mallin, 2005; Onyemah, 2003; Swanson, 2003); however, none of the research was focused on sales organizations in the pharmaceutical industry. Lopez (2000) examined the influence of management control systems on the implementation of market-oriented and customer-oriented strategies in the retail industry; the study found an association between behavior-based control and the implementation of market-oriented and customer-oriented strategies among sales personnel. Mallin (2005) tested an integrated framework that combined control and trust in sales governance; the sample of sales managers from a variety of industries employed behavior-based control more frequently than outcome-based control. An association was discovered for sales management control, trust, and sales performance, but the sample of sales managers did not include sales managers from sales organizations in the pharmaceutical industry.

Onyemah's (2003) evidence asserted that firms used inconsistent systems of sales force management control and, because of the inconsistencies, salesperson performance was negatively influenced directly and indirectly via role conflict. The sample from the study included a large number of diverse firms located throughout the world. Swanson (2003) investigated the dimensions of individual salesperson performance and developed taxonomy of individual sales behaviors. Consistent with the research in peer-reviewed

34

journals, limited dissertation research was focused on examining sales management control constructs in sales organizations within the pharmaceutical industry. The present study will attempt to close the gap in the empirical research about sales management control in the pharmaceutical industry.

Salesperson Performance Research

Attempts to answer the question of what makes a good salesperson have a 70-year history of empirical research (Churchill et al., 1985). Despite the volume of research about the issue, questions remain unanswered with respect to the predictors of sales performance, which dimensions should be measured, and how those dimensions should be measured. Walker et al. (1979) stated that, "Sales performance is the result of carrying out a number of discrete and specific activities which may vary greatly across different types of selling jobs and situations" (p. 22).

Empirical research about sales performance dates back to the work of Oschrin (1918). Conceptual approaches to sales performance, at least from a normative perspective, date back even further. Plank and Dempsey (1980) mentioned that formula selling dates back to William James in 1898 and need-satisfaction selling dates back to Strong in 1925. Past sales performance research tended to draw on survey research. Other data collection techniques, such as focus groups, were used less often.

Sales managers have attempted to understand and explain predictors of sales performance (Churchill et al., 1985). According to Churchill et al. (1985), studies about sales performance yielded inconsistent results with respect to such forecasts. These studies have also yielded inconsistent results with respect to the strength of the relationship between sales performance and performance predictors. In a meta-analysis to analyze factors affecting salesperson performance, Churchill et al. found that no single predictor could explain the significant variation in sales performance amongst sales representatives and concluded that no single factor or even several factors in a single category of predictors could accurately predict salespeople's future sales performance. In addition, Churchill et al. developed theoretical models with multiple determinants and discovered that categories of salesperson performance were more accurate for explaining organizational sales performance. Whether the shortfalls found in the meta-analysis by Churchill et al. represent improper performance factors, incorrect choices of performance dimensions, or unreliable performance measures remains uncertain.

Seminal empirical research about sales performance can be divided into two primary conceptual perspectives: Walker et al. (1977, 1979) and Weitz (1978, 1979, 1981). Walker et al. (1977, 1979) developed an expectancy motivation model of sales performance. The researchers originally formulated the model without explicit reference to sales behavior. In 1979, the original model was modified explicitly by including selling behaviors, executing those behaviors in the model, and distinguishing those behaviors from overall selling effectiveness.

The Walker Expectancy Motivation Framework

The expectancy motivational framework developed by Walker et al. (1977, 1979) suggested direct relationships existed for five sets of variables: (a) personal, organizational, and environmental factors; (b) motivation; (c) aptitude; (d) skill level; and (e) role perceptions, sales behaviors, and performance. Personal, organizational, and environmental factors were understood to moderate the relationship between behavioral performance and overall sales effectiveness. Drawing from organizational psychology,

Walker et al. (1979) defined behavior as "What people do (the tasks they expend effort on) in the course of working" (p. 33).

Behavior with respect to sales, therefore, involves the execution of selling-related activities by salespeople in the performance of their jobs. Performance represents behavior that is evaluated in terms of its contribution to the goals of the organization (Walker et al., 1979). In addition, performance embodies a normative aspect that reflects whether the salesperson behavior is "good" or "bad" (p. 35) relative to an organization's goals and objectives. Walker et al. described sales organization effectiveness as a composite index of organizational outcomes for which individual salespeople are only partially responsible. Unlike performance, sales organization effectiveness is not directly related to salesperson behavior; sales organization effectiveness constitutes one among many factors not controlled by the salesperson, such as management polices and territory potential.

Expectancy Framework Research

A review by Churchill et al. (1985) identified 116 empirical articles that could be examined within the Walker et al. (1979) framework. The meta-analytic review revealed relatively low associations between predictors of performance within the Walker et al. model and overall sales performance. The notion of sales behaviors, as Churchill et al. (1985) noted, was not examined in the study.

One empirical study cited Walker et al.'s (1979) perspective about sales behaviors: Avila, Fern, and Mann (1988) attempted to address the relationship of sales behaviors to some notion of sales performance and effectiveness. Avila et al. examined sales behavior using seven single-item measures of behavior in a two-company cross-sectional modeling exercise. Sales behaviors were hypothesized to be related to both overall performance assessment and goal achievement. Goal achievement was defined as the percentage of quota and net gain in accounts and represented a measure of effectiveness as defined by Walker et al. (1979).

The salesperson's manager measured performance as a qualitative assessment of overall performance. The measures used by Avila et al. (1988) reflected Walker et al.'s (1979) conceptualization of sales effectiveness as opposed to sales performance: Overall performance was portrayed as a multidimensional concept. Results from the Avila et al. study suggested single measures do not provide strong explanations for overall performance. In addition, Avila et al. recommended that salespeople not be evaluated with criteria beyond their control. Finally, Avila et al. proposed that sales behaviors are linked to performance.

Several articles have attempted to create overall performance indicators of sales effectiveness from a behavioral perspective. The first attempt to create performance indicators was made by Behrman and Perreault (1982) who developed a self-report performance scale based on responses from 200 salespeople and 42 sales managers at five industrial firms. Based on the content review and sub-sample item analysis, the initial item pool of 65 items over seven performance measures was reduced to 31 individual items, representing the following five aspects of sales performance: sales objectives, technical knowledge, provision of information, control of expenses, and sales presentations.

In an extension of the Behrman and Perreault (1982) study, Lagace and Howe (1988) suggested that the items on the scale were more appropriate for measuring the performance of industrial salespeople than retail salespeople. Bush, Bush, Ortinau, and Hair (as cited in Plank & Reid, 1994) developed a scale for retail salespeople based on retail selling behaviors. The Bush et al. scale consisted of 22 individual items grouped into performance categories: merchandise procedures, sales and customer service ability, knowledge of store policy and procedures, and product-merchandise knowledge. For both studies, the individual items as well as the broader factors represented sales behaviors as defined by Walker et al. (1977).

The Weitz Contingency Perspective

The other major conceptual perspective employed when examining sales performance and effectiveness is Weitz's (1979) contingency framework. Weitz (1978, 1979, 1981) and Weitz et al. (1986) noted the importance of the sales process and proposed adaptiveness as a framework for examining the nature of the process. According to the adaptive selling perspective, sales behaviors are important predictors of sales effectiveness. In fact, the seminal work by Weitz (1981) suggested much of the research about sales performance has been contradictory or inconclusive because of attempts to generalize over too wide a range of too difficult-to-define situations. Weitz et al. (1986) suggested a contingency framework for defining sales effectiveness across customer interactions as a function of resources allocated to the salesperson, the dynamics of the buying-task, and the relationship between customer and salesperson and interactions among these variables. The term customer interactions, as employed by Weitz (1981), can refer to a single face-to-face encounter or a sequence of face-to-face interactions.

In developing a model, Weitz (1981) narrowly defined four types of sales behaviors: (a) adapting to customers, (b) establishing influence base, (c) using influencing techniques, and (d) controlling the sales interaction. These behaviors directly influence sales effectiveness, but the impact of these influences is moderated by the relationships between the salesperson and customer, salesperson resources, and the characteristic of the buying task. The appropriateness and effectiveness of the various behaviors is affected by the particular sales situation.

The sales situation, as described in earlier work by Weitz (1979), is the environment in which a salesperson operates. These sales situations can be described in terms of two sets of characteristics: the characteristic of the customer's buying task and the salesperson-customer relationship (Weitz, 1981). Characteristics of the salesperson-customer relationship include the level of conflict, the level of bargaining, relative power, the nature of the customer's need and beliefs, and the customer's knowledge of available alternatives. The sales situation, as reflected by these two sets of characteristics, moderates the effectiveness of various types of selling behaviors.

Sales effectiveness is defined as "The degree in which the 'preferred solutions' of salespeople are realized across their customer interactions" (Weitz, 1981 p. 91). Weitz did not provide an explicit operational definition for a measure of sales effectiveness. Work by Weitz et al. (1986) expanded the conceptual model of contingency or adaptive behavior by incorporating knowledge and motivation into the model. The central focus of the extension was that adaptive selling behavior leads to performance and adaptive selling behavior is influenced by a number of sales management variables that operate through a set of mediator variables.

In what represents an early contingency paradigm, Pasold (1975) developed a questionnaire that categorized salesperson behaviors as reactive, preactive, interactive, and proactive. The study tested different behavior patterns under different environmental conditions and found that the appropriateness of various behavior patterns differed across different environments. Later work defined the notion of adaptive selling more fully: Giacobbe (1991) included adjustments in strategy and tactics, social style and personality, verbal communication styles, and physical appearance. Both the effect of adaptive selling on salesperson performance and the influence of empathetic ability and cue perception on adaptive selling ability were studied, but Giacobbe found no evidence of an influence for either empathy or cue perception for adaptive selling behavior.

Research by Spiro and Weitz (1990) suggested that salespeople differ in their abilities to adapt within sales presentations. Adaptiveness could be viewed as an aptitude leading to a skill within the Walker et al. (1979) framework. Weitz et al. (1986) and others have suggested that an understanding of salesperson's selling-related knowledge can provide valuable insights into the differences between sales effectiveness and performance. For example, Leigh and McGraw (1989), using script theory, found that experienced salespeople with more sophisticated knowledge structures behave differently to less experienced salespeople.

According to Leigh and McGraw (1989), experienced salespeople with increased knowledge performed better than did less experienced salespeople with limited knowledge. Work by Sujan, Sujan, and Bettman (1988) found that knowledge structures predict better sales performance for less experienced salespeople. Finally, Szymanski

(1988) proposed declarative knowledge, or the ability to classify and meet the customer's needs at each stage of the sales process, as a key sales behavior for successful salespeople. In summary, most existing sales performance research has not examined behavior directly. Only limited research has been directed toward understanding sales behaviors and their influence on sales performance. Past research has suggested sales behaviors are important predictors of salesperson performance.

Sales Behaviors

Walker et al. (1979) defined sales behavior as "What people do (the tasks they expend effort on) in the course of working" (p. 33). Sales behaviors involve the execution of selling-related activities by salespeople in the performance of their jobs. Examples of sales behaviors include planning sales calls, filling out call reports, asking questions during a sales call, providing answers to a prospect's questions, and taking a buyer to lunch. According to Walker et al., these sales behaviors must be completed successfully to achieve assigned sales goals.

Much of the limited research on sales behavior has centered on identifying the behaviors associated with different types of sales positions. For example, an early study by Lamont and Lundstrom (1974) examined sales behaviors in the building materials industry by factor analyzing 60 items and identifying eight general or behavioral dimensions associated with industrial sales positions. The eight behavioral dimensions were assisting and working with district management, customer service, personal integrity and selling ethics, direct selling, developing relationships with customers, keeping abreast of market conditions, meeting sales objectives, and maintaining complete customer records.

Similarly, Behrman and Perreault (1982) developed a measure of sales performance incorporating the notion of types of sales behaviors believed to be the major job responsibilities of most industrial salespersons. Their analysis resulted in 31 individual behavioral items representing five aspects of industrial sales performance. A study by Moore, Eckrich, and Carlson (1986) examined the importance of 82 selling competencies, many of which are analogous to selling behaviors as they relate to performance for manufacturer salespeople, distributor salespeople, and manufacturers' agents.

Moncrief (1986) presented seminal research about classifying sales behaviors and identified types of sales positions based on the quantity of behaviors salespeople performed. Based on a survey of the literature, Moncrief identified 21 activities or behaviors that are involved in selling. Data on the behaviors of 1,393 salespeople representing 51 companies were factor analyzed and yielded 10 job factors. Cluster analysis, based on factor scores, was employed to develop taxonomy of industrial sales positions.

Attempts to improve sales performance and effectiveness have focused on identifying predictors of an individual salesperson's performance. The results of these studies (Churchill et al., 1985; Mount & Barrick, 1995; Vinchur et al., 1998) have resulted in low levels of explanatory power. Much of the past research explored the individual characteristics or behaviors of salespeople as potential predictors of performance. While the influence of other variables that are not controlled by the salesperson is recognized, limited research has been directed at these factors. Moreover, only a few studies (Babakus et al., 1996; Grant & Cravens, 1996; Piercy et al., 1999) have examined the sales manager level of organizations. None of these studies (Babakus et al., 1996; Cravens et al., 1993; Darmon, 1993; Ganesan et al., 1993; Grant & Cravens, 1996; Oliver & Anderson, 1994; Piercy et al., 1999; Weitz et al., 1986) examined salespeople or sales management within the pharmaceutical industry.

Researchers and sales executives recognize the importance of situational contingencies, including systems of sales management control and sales territory design, as moderators and/or predictors of the performance of salespeople and effectiveness of sales organizations (Babakus et al., 1996). The next four sections of the literature review examine sales management control and sales territory design as possible moderators and/or predictors of salesperson performance and effectiveness in sales organizations.

Management Control

Control mechanisms are central to the efficient and effective functioning of organizations (Barker & Jennings, 1999). Controlling is recognized as one of the major activities of managers and is generally viewed as an integral link for connecting other essential managerial functions such as planning, organizing, and leading. According to Barker and Jennings, the control process ensures that actual and planned activities are congruent with each other. The control process includes monitoring organized efforts, comparing progress with planned objectives, and making the necessary decisions to ensure success. Potential benefits of effective control processes, in terms of performance enhancement, are effectively designed and controls implemented.

According to Tannenbaum (1968), management control consists of directing the daily sales activities of the salesperson. Several other researchers have identified planning as a key element of management control (Dutton, 1925; Lichtner, 1924). Reeves and

44

Woodard (1970) argued the proper domains of management control include direction of daily activities, evaluation of sales results, and analyzing goal versus actual performance to identify and correct any deviations. In addition, the compensation plan is a common method used to control and motivate salespeople (Churchill, Ford, & Walker, 1979; Cooke, 1999).

Literature about management control makes a distinction between formal and informal management control mechanisms. Formal controls are written, management-initiated mechanisms especially aimed at influencing salespersons' activities in the desired direction (Jaworski, 1988). Informal controls, such as unwritten, worker-initiated mechanisms, influence salespersons' self-control behaviors (Lawler, 1976), clan control (Ouchi, 1979), or cultural control (Wilkins & Ouchi, 1983).

Flamholtz, Das, and Tsui (1985) observed that control research has evolved mainly from three theoretical traditions: sociological, administrative, and psychological. The sociological tradition focuses on applying formal rules and the power of authority to govern and supervise employees. According to Weber (1947), in modern management thought, authority is based upon rational grounds and is presented in the form of impersonal bureaucratic systems. Flamholtz et al. (1985) observed that management control involves structural mechanisms of rules, policies, and a chain of command.

The administrative tradition is interested in using managerial skills and techniques to supervise actions and direct the behaviors of individuals (Davis, 1934). These management skills and techniques are derived from the earlier management principles of Cornell (1928) and Davis (1934). These principles include planning, preparation, scheduling, dispatching, direction, supervision, comparison, and correction (Giglioni & Bedeian, 1974).

Finally, the psychological tradition stresses human cognitive capacities and individuals' attitudinal reactions. Researchers in the psychological tradition have devoted attention to the concepts of goal setting; intrinsic and extrinsic motivation; and the perceptions of and reactions to rewards, feedback, and interpersonal communications (Flamholtz et al., 1985; Lawler, 1973; Tannenbaum, 1968).

Because different approaches have been used to study the phenomenon of control, an integrative view was adopted in order to conceptualize systems of sales management control. The integrative view suggests that systems of sales management control consist of elements from each of the three traditions, namely, sociological, administrative, and psychological. The elements of formal policies, rules, and procedures are from the sociological tradition; the elements of measurement and evaluation are representative of the administrative tradition; and the elements of goal setting and using rewards and feedback are from the psychological tradition.

Systems of sales management control are defined in the present study as an aggregate set of policies, procedures, and rules sales organizations use to supervise, guide, assess, and compensate the activities of salespeople (Anderson & Oliver, 1987). The current definition is consistent with other conceptualizations in the literature. For example, Jaworski (1988) suggested that formal controls such as written, management-initiated mechanisms influence the probability that employee and group behavior will support stated marketing objectives.

The control system definition advanced in the present study is different from the concept of leadership. The distinction lies in control systems' practice of an integrated approach to supervise, guide, assess, and compensate activities of employees; leadership is centered upon the employment of personal influence on the part of superiors.

In summary, different perspectives have been adopted to examine systems of sales management control. Based on the analysis of research about systems of management control, various definitions of systems of management control contain the following common elements (Flamholtz et al., 1985):

1. Monitoring element: The use of the authority of management to detect a salesperson's work-related behavior

2. Direction element: Predetermined rules and standards to direct salespeople in the attainment of desirable goals

3. Evaluation element: Various forms of performance appraisal processes to judge salespeople's performance against select criteria

4. Reward element: Tangible and/or intangible incentives and rewards to reinforce salespeople's desired outcomes.

Theories of Sales Management Control

Sales force governance has been analyzed with the frameworks of several economic theories, especially agency theory and transaction cost analysis. Anderson (1985) published one of the first empirical studies testing agency theory and addressed the exchange management must make between home sales forces, employees, and independent agents. Most of the predictions of transaction cost analysis (Williamson, 1975, 1981) were supported by empirical research (John & Weitz, 1989) that asserted

47

that as salesperson performance becomes more difficult to assess, an increased probability emerges that firms will use a directly controlled sales force rather than commission-motivated sales force.

Anderson and Oliver (1987) considered the implications of transaction cost analysis as well as other theories, such as agency theory, organization theory (Ouchi, 1979), and cognitive evaluation theory (Deci, 1975) for applying a specific control philosophy. Agency theory appears to provide an attractive framework for sales force control analysis (Eisenhardt, 1985) as it addresses the problem of how principals can control agents to whom they delegate decision-making authority. Principals and agents are assumed to pursue different goals and frequently not to share the same information level or asymmetry. Information asymmetry exists within sale force control because salespersons typically have better information about their own territory sales response functions than management does (Lal & Staelin, 1986).

According to agency theory, when information asymmetry exists between principal and agent, the principal must determine the optimal approach to control agent behavior (Eisenhardt, 1985). Principals can control agents by observing their activities or outcomes. According to Eisenhardt, outcome controls are associated with environmental uncertainties. These environmental uncertainties increase the chances that proper activities may not yield expected results. In this case, agency theory supports compensating agents for increased risk.

According to Basu, Srinvason, and Staelin (1985), several authors have applied agency theory to determine what compensation plan structure for sales forces will optimally control salespeople's activities and, consequently, outcomes. The literature is

48

based on the assumption that compensation is the best way to control salespeople's activities. However, Basu et al. argued that compensation is only one of several tools toward achieving this goal.

Whether considered through agency theory or transaction cost analysis, circumstances can be identified under which a firm should select a behavior-based or an outcome-based sales force control philosophy. Anderson and Oliver (1987) proposed a control system positioned somewhere on a continuum ranging from purely behavior-based to purely outcome-based. Outcome-based control systems monitor the final outputs and require minimal salesperson supervision, simple performance measures, and compensation plans. Outcome-based control is liberal management whereby salespersons are independent entrepreneurs responsible for their own activities and performance. In contrast, behavior-based controls monitor intermediate steps in the process. Behavior-based control requires close salesperson supervision, supervisors' interference with salespeople's activities, and more complex and subjective evaluation of salespersons' performance (Oliver & Anderson, 1987).

Stathakopoulos (1996) attempted to synthesize three theories underlying sales force control. In order to predict the effectiveness of different types of control, Stathakopoulos applied selected constructs from organizational theories such as outcome observables, behavior observables, and transaction specific assets. Stathakopoulos' theoretical framework has not been validated empirically.

Systems of Sales Management Control

Anderson and Oliver (1987) defined a systems of sales force control as the set of procedures for supervising, guiding, assessing, and compensating the activities of

49

salespeople. Some such systems focus on results, known as outcome-based control systems, and others focus on inputs and processes, known as behavior-based control systems. According to Stanton and Buskirk (1983), training, motivation, coaching, support, and compensation of salespeople can be conceived of as part of overall sales force control. Stanton and Buskirk suggested sales force controls are pervasive and related to most aspects of sales management.

An outcome-based control system guides salespeople's behavior by emphasizing their outcomes rather than their sales activities and processes (Anderson & Oliver, 1987). In an outcome-based control system, limited management supervision and direction of salespeople occur. According to Anderson and Oliver, "Outcome-based control approximates a market contracting arrangement wherein salespeople are left alone to achieve results in their own way using their own strategies" (p. 76). Managers exercise little control over non-sales behavior because an outcome-based control system relies on market mechanisms to direct salespeople (John & Weitz, 1989; Ouchi, 1979).

Outcome-based control systems employ objective measures, such as sales volumes, revenues, and sales quotas (Oliver & Anderson, 1995). In an outcome-based control system, compensation and reward policies are primarily contingent on the sales results or outcomes of the salesperson. According to Cravens et al. (1993), when the system of sales force control is outcome-based, field sales management supervise and direct the activities of salespeople to a lesser extent, use objective measures of outcomes to evaluate performance, and compensate salespeople with higher proportions of incentive compensation.

50

In contrast, a behavior-based control system places greater emphasis on job inputs such as activities, sales strategies, and personal qualities (Oliver & Anderson, 1987). According to Oliver and Anderson, "A behavior-based control system is typified by high levels of supervisor monitoring, direction, and intervention in activities" (p. 77). In addition, a behavior-based control system is subject to complex methods of evaluating performance due to reliance on measuring sales inputs that demand objective quantification. Consequently, management must provide a significant amount of subjective managerial feedback about selling and non-selling activities within behavior-based control systems. A behavior-based control system is consistent with a bureaucratic mechanism in which superiors who manage subordinates use close surveillance and extensive performance measures (Ouchi, 1979). A compensation and reward policy in a behavior-based control system is more focused on salary than commission (John & Weitz, 1989).

Although the two control systems are based on different managerial philosophies, they may be used at once in the same organization (Anderson & Oliver, 1987; Ouchi & Maguire, 1975). According to Oliver and Anderson (1995), few sales firms use only a single system for sales force control; instead, most companies have adopted a hybrid approach by combining different degrees of behavior-based and outcome-based control tools and techniques.

Research about Control Systems for Sales Management

Anderson and Oliver (1987) developed seven research propositions about important relationships between the types of control systems emphasized for sales forces and cognitions and capabilities, affects and attitudes, motivation, behavioral strategies, and performance of sales forces. The first proposition focused on control system strategies. According to Anderson and Oliver, in behavior-based control systems, salespeople are monitored more closely, subject to considerable direction, evaluated on an input basis by subjective and more complex measures, and rewarded with a higher proportion of fixed compensation. In outcome-based control systems, salespeople are monitored less frequently, offered little direction, evaluated on outcome measures by objective and simple methods, and rewarded with a higher proportion of incentive compensation.

The second proposition theorized that the more a control system is behavior-based rather than outcome-based, the more product knowledge, company knowledge, and integrated sales expertise the salesperson has, and the more professionally competent the salesperson will be (Anderson & Oliver, 1987). The third proposition argued that if a control system is behavior-based rather than outcome-based, a salesperson will identify with and feel committed to the sales organization, be willing to accept direction and cooperate as part of sales team, accept the authority of management, and welcome management performance reviews.

The fourth proposition focused on salesperson motivation. According to Anderson and Oliver (1987), where a control system is behavior-based rather than outcome-based, the salesperson has higher levels of intrinsic motivation, is motivated by peer recognition, and is motivated to serve the sales agency. The fifth proposition suggested salespeople's hierarchy of motivation differs across outcome-based and behavior-based systems. According to Anderson and Oliver, in behavior-based systems, the agency's interest comes first because the agency shelters the salesperson from risk and, by active monitoring, forms a strong communication bond with salespeople. Customers and principals ranked next in the hierarchy because neither offers the direction, authority, and risk assumption by the agency.

The sixth proposition focused on salesperson behavioral strategies. Anderson and Oliver (1987) argued that in the case of a behavioral-based rather than outcome-based control system, a salesperson can be expected to plan for each call, make fewer calls, operate at a lower ratio of selling to non-selling time, and spend more time on sales support activities. The seventh proposition analyzed salesperson performance. According to Anderson and Oliver, in control systems that is more behavioral-based than outcome-based, individual salespeople will come closer to achieving the sales agency's goals and to serving customer needs but will perform more poorly on traditional output measures of individual level performance.

Cravens et al. (1993) developed the first conceptual model depicting relationships amongst control system for sales forces, sale force characteristics, sales force performance, and sales organization effectiveness as a framework for testing the propositions formulated by Anderson and Oliver (1987). Cravens et al. (1993) integrated Anderson and Oliver's (1987) propositions into the model by developing specific hypotheses of relationships between the type of system of sales force control and other model constructs. Craven et al.'s (1993) methodology included a sample of sales managers from 144 diverse sales organizations. The types of sales organizations included companies dealing in industrial products, industrial services, consumer products, and consumer services. Cravens et al. viewed managerial control and the control implicit in the compensation scheme as independent control mechanisms, in contrast to Anderson and Oliver's (1987) view that they are interconnected.

The results from the study by Cravens et al. (1993) provided support for the relationship between behavior-based systems for sales force control and specific sales force characteristics, different dimensions of sales force performance, and sales organization effectiveness. Cravens et al.'s suggested a limited role for incentive compensation in sales force control systems and the need for a proper blend between field sales management and compensation control. These findings are in accord with Anderson and Oliver's (1987) propositions.

Another empirical study for testing Anderson and Oliver's (1987) propositions was published by Oliver and Anderson (1994). They developed a comprehensive formal control measure based on their seminal work and constructed a control index consisting of six dimensions: the extent of emphasis on supervision, results, attitude, effort, information feedback, and percentage of salary in total compensation of salespeople. The 23 items in the control index were considered formative indicators representing the control system with outcome-based and behavior-based control as opposites.

Based on research recommendations from Cravens et al. (1993) to control for environmental variation by conducting research on several sales organizations in the same industry, Oliver and Anderson (1994) changed the study methodology to include a sample of salespersons from multiple firms in the electronics industry. In addition, they tested a hybrid model of management and compensation control. To test their hybrid model, they developed an index of sales force control with compensation as a measurable component. The study results were consistent with the behavior-based versus outcome-based control consequences proposed in the Anderson and Oliver (1987) framework. Perceptions of a behavior-based control governance structure appeared to be related to greater effect and acceptance amongst sales representatives as well as suggested some tendency for increased professional competence, intrinsic motivation, and attendance to agency goals at the expense of other goals (Oliver & Anderson, 1994). In contrast to Oliver and Anderson's expectations, the salesperson's chosen behavioral strategy was not affected by the control system the salesperson perceived was being employed. Oliver and Anderson suggested that outcome control perceptions coincide with extrinsic motivation and pointed to a strong correlation between behavior-based control and organization commitment of salespeople. However, the research findings failed to demonstrate clear and consistent effects on reported time allocation behavior.

Although Cravens et al. (1993) and Oliver and Andersons' (1994) studies used somewhat different methodologies and procedures, both reached similar conclusions. The main conclusions are that empirical evidence tends to support Anderson and Oliver's (1987) theoretical propositions. In particular, behavior-based controls tend to be positively associated with affective states, such as commitment to the firm, acceptance of authority, cooperation within a selling team, acceptance of evaluation systems, and risk aversion, as well as with salespeople's intrinsic motivation. An unexpected conclusion from Oliver and Anderson's (1994) research was that control system orientation is not related to salespeople's selling strategies. Consistent with Cravens et al. (1993), Oliver and Anderson (1994) acknowledged that although meaningful findings emerged from their investigation, the overall level of findings resulted in low levels of explanatory power. The study settings did not include sales organizations within the pharmaceutical industry.

In another study, Oliver and Anderson (1995) extended their work. Acknowledging that the study results from their previous research (Oliver & Anderson, 1994) were weak although statistically significant, Oliver and Anderson (1995) provided the plausible explanation that firms could possibly use opposite control philosophies simultaneously, such as compensating salespersons with straight salaries and providing only loose supervision. Other researchers (Jaworski, 1988; Ouchi & Maguire, 1975) had previously proposed and observed these hybrid forms of control. Oliver and Anderson (1995) suggested that organizations could potentially benefit from using both forms of management control systems simultaneously. However, the level of explanatory power demonstrated by research about hybrid forms of sales management control was low.

In line with the Anderson and Oliver's (1987) control conceptualizations, Babakus et al. (1996) operationalized strategies for sales management control as the degree of a sales manager's supervision, guidance, assessment, and compensation of salespeople. In contrast to previous research, the Babakus et al., scale include 25 items that reflected four control dimensions. The four control dimensions included sales management control, sales territory design, sales force performance, and sales organization effectiveness. The items comprising the scales for measuring the control dimensions display several similarities with the Oliver and Anderson (1994) measures.

The conceptual model (see Figure 1) guiding Babakus et al.'s (1996) research extended and integrated several research studies about sales management control. Consistent with prior research about sales management control (Cravens et al., 1993;

56

Oliver & Anderson, 1994), Babakus et al. examined the relationship of systems of sales management control, both behavior-based and outcome-based, on sales organization effectiveness. However, they expanded the conceptual model by adding sales territory design.

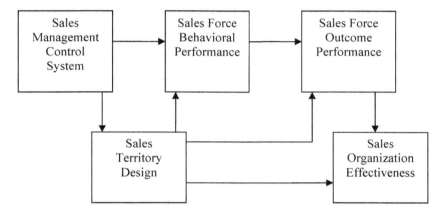

Figure 1. Sales organization design framework.

Note: From "Investigating the relationships among sales management control, sales territory design, salesperson performance, and sales organizational effectiveness," by E. Babakus, D. W. Cravens, K. Grant, T. N. Ingram, and R. W. LaForge, 1996, *International Journal of Research in Marketing, 13*(4), p. 353. Copyright 1996 by Elsevier Publishing. Reprinted with permission of the author.

The research method used by Babakus et al. (1996) included a study of sales organizations from diverse companies to test specific hypotheses developed from the conceptual model. The types of sales organizations comprising the sample included generalists, product or service specialists, and customer specialists. Consumer products represented the largest portion of the sales for 58% of the companies in the sample compared to 7% consumer services (Babakus et al., 1996). Industrial products accounted for 28% of the firms' sales, compared to 7% for industrial services (Babakus et al., 1996). The sample did not include sales organizations within the pharmaceutical industry. Data were collected by means of a mail questionnaire completed by company sales executives and first-line sales managers in each participating company. The field sales teams supervised by the sales managers served as the unit of analysis for the study. The sales organizations were located in Australia (Babakus et al., 1996).

The empirical results (see Table 1) from first-line sales managers provided strong support that a company's system of sales management control had a positive influence on sales organization effectiveness through sales force behavior-based and outcome-based performance and through sales territory design (Babakus et al., 1996). The relative size of the standard coefficients indicated that systems of sales management control are related to both sales territory design and behavior performance. According to Babakus et al., the coefficients for the management control system and sales territory design on behavior-based performance were similar in magnitude. Moreover, the hypothesized antecedents explained substantial proportions of variance in behavioral performance, outcome performance, and effectiveness.

The study results (Babakus et al, 1996) also indicated that sales territory design had a positive relationship with behavior-based and outcome-based performance. In addition, the results indicated that sales management control is related to both sales territory design and behavior-based performance. Moreover, sales territory design has a similar effect on both behavior-based and outcome-based performance. According to Babakus et al., behavior-based performance has a significant influence on outcome-based performance.

Table 1.

ML Estimates of Structural Parameters and Model Statistic (Field Sales Manager Sample N = 146)[a]

Model parameters	Hypothesis	Parameter definition	Standardized coefficient	t-value
γ_{21}	*H3*	Activities $\rightarrow$ behavior	0.222	2.25
β_{32}	*H1*	Behavior $\rightarrow$ outcome	0.653	5.96
γ_{11}	*H4*	Activities $\rightarrow$ design	0.356	3.91
β_{21}	*H6*	Design $\rightarrow$ behavior	0.279	2.76
β_{31}	*H7*	Design $\rightarrow$ outcome	0.234	2.98
β_{43}	*H2*	Outcome $\rightarrow$ effect	0.502	4.20
β_{41}	*H5*	Design $\rightarrow$ effect	0.245	2.17

Note:[a] $\chi^2 = 180.99$; *df* = 85; *p*-value = 0.000; NFI = 0.82; GFI = 0.863; RMSR = 0.073; NFI-2 = 0.90; AGFI = 0.807. Variance explained (R^2) in: Design (η_1) = 0.127; Behavior (η_2) = 0.171; Outcome (η_3) = 0.591; Effectiveness (η_4) = 0.428. From "Investigating the relationships among sales management control, sales territory design, salesperson performance, and sales organizational effectiveness," by E. Babakus, D. W. Cravens, K. Grant, T. N. Ingram, and R. W. LaForge, 1996, *International Journal of Research in Marketing, 13*(4), p. 355. Copyright 1996 by Elsevier Publishing. Reprinted with permission of the author.

Challagalla and Shervani (1996) modified prior conceptualizations of control systems. Unlike other research, Challagalla and Shervani's model adopted the term supervisory controls instead of formal control systems to denote various elements of sales control measures. Specifically, three different categories of supervisory controls were proposed: output controls, activity controls, and capacity controls. In addition, each category of supervisory control included three dimensions, information, reward, and punishment, resulting in nine forms of supervisory controls: output information, output rewards, output punishments, activity information, activity rewards, activity punishments, capability information, capability rewards, and capability punishments.

The latter classification of controls focused on three key aspects of control systems: output, activity, and capability. In each of these three aspects, sales managers may use information, reward, and punishment to reinforce or discourage certain behavior and activities of employees. For example, activity information refers to "specifying routine activity goals, monitoring salespeople, and providing feedback on activity performance" (Challagalla & Shervani, 1996, p. 91). Activity rewards refers to applying rewards to promote behaviors consistent with managerial expectations. The output controls in the latter model are similar to the outcome-based control system posited by Anderson and Oliver (1987), while activity and capability controls appear to be an extension of the behavior-based control system posited by Anderson and Oliver. Challagalla and Shervani (1996) found that output, activity, and capability control were positively related to satisfaction with a supervisor.

The latter classification of controls focuses on three key aspects of control systems: output, activity, and capability. In each of these three aspects, sales managers may use information, reward, and punishment to reinforce or discourage certain behaviors and activities of employees. For example, *activity information* refers to "specifying routine activity goals, monitoring salespeople, and providing feedback on activity performance" (Challagalla & Shervani, 1996, p. 91). *Activity rewards* refer to applying rewards to promote behaviors consistent with managerial expectations. The output controls in the latter model are similar to the outcome-based control system posited by Anderson and Oliver (1987), while activity and capability controls appear to be an extension of the behavior-based control system posited by Anderson and Oliver. Challagalla and Shervani (1996) found that output, activity, and capability control positively related to satisfaction with supervisor.

While Anderson and Oliver's (1987) framework of outcome-based versus behavior-based control systems has received recognition in sales and marketing literature, other marketing researchers have also made contributions in this domain (Baldauf et al., 2005). For example, Jaworski (1988) proposed a theoretical model that identified the determinants and consequences of the controls in use. Some characteristics of Jaworski's framework are significant. First, the theoretical framework considers both an organization's external and internal environments as critical factors that may affect the choice of control systems. Second, control systems are separated into two categories: formal controls and informal controls. Formal controls include input controls, process controls, and output controls, whereas informal controls are comprised of social controls, cultural controls, and self-controls. Finally, Jaworski explicitly indicated that environmental variables are likely to moderate the link between control systems and organizational and/or individual consequences.

According to Piercy, Cravens, and Lane (2003), gender differences with respect to behavior and outcomes of salespeople has attracted considerable research attention. A strong consensus has emerged that few gender differences exist with respect to various salesperson job-related perceptions (Moncrief, Babakus, Cravens, & Jenkins, 2000; Piercy et al., 2003; Ramaswami, 2002). The results of a single company study (Piercy, Cravens, & Lane, 2001) suggested a relationship between a sales manager's gender and

61

sales team performance. The results of their study revealed that salespersons managed by female managers exhibited higher sales manager behavior control activities, increased job satisfaction, increased job participation, increased role clarity, lower job anxiety and burnout, higher organizational commitment, and a lower propensity to leave. The findings from the single-company study can be compared to Comer, Jolson, Dubinsky, and Yammarino's (1995) research, which determined differences in the use of management control and revealed that salesperson perceptions of control reflect sales manager gender.

Piercy et al. (2003) investigated gender differences amongst sales managers within multiple companies. The purpose of their study was to explore these gender differences from the viewpoint of the sales manager. The results of their study confirmed the generalizability of certain findings in previous gender research (Comer et al., 1995) and lent confidence to the results of the single-company research performed by Piercy et al. (2001). The results suggested sales teams directed by female managers exhibited increased levels of effectiveness. Female sales managers exhibited a higher competency level in behavior-based control activities compared to their male counterparts (Piercy et al., 2003).

Piercy et al. (2004) conducted sales management and compensation control research in developing countries. The research was conducted in Greece, India, and Malaysia. The objective of the research was to understand the consequences of sales management and compensation-based control strategies employed by organizations within these countries. According to Piercy et al., a limited amount of international research exists on the topic. The conceptual model examined relationships among several of the sales management control variables identified by Anderson and Oliver (1987). The conceptual framework used by Piercy et al. (2004) was consistent with the Babakus et al. (1996) study; however, Piercy et al. (2004) measured sales management and compensation control as separate constructs.

The findings from research focused on developing countries (Piercy et al., 2004) did not support previous theories and research about sales management control (Cravens et al., 1993). Study results from the study by Piercy et al. (2004) suggested that combining incentive pay and behavioral control positively influenced salesperson and organizational outcomes. The implications of Piercy et al.'s findings contradicted the existing conceptual logic in previous research by Cravens et al. (1993): The combination of both high levels of incentive pay and behavior-based control appeared to reduce salesperson and organizational effectiveness. The sample in Piercy et al.'s (2004) research included field sales managers from various companies and industries who directly supervised salespeople involved in business-to-business selling situations; pharmaceutical companies were not included.

Baldauf et al. (2005) completed a synthesis of research about sales management control. According to Baldauf et al., existing knowledge on marketing and research about sales management control is based on two seminal conceptual developments. First, Anderson and Oliver (1987), drawing from theoretical approaches in economics, organizational behavior, and psychology, conceptualized a formal management control framework. They formulated propositions about the consequences that either a behavior-based or outcome-based system of sales force control can have on salespersons' cognitions and capabilities, affects and attitudes, motivation, behavioral strategies, and performance. Second, Jaworski (1988) proposed a conceptualization consisting of formal and informal dimensions of management control for marketing personnel.

The resulting research propositions were rooted in the management and accounting disciplines and were concerned with the antecedents and consequences of formal and informal control. According to Baldauf et al. (2005), no apparent unified view exists of sales management control. Moreover, the two primary conceptualizations (Anderson & Oliver, 1987; Jaworski, 1988) have resulted in different measurement approaches.

Sales Management Control Research in the Pharmaceutical Industry

Futrell, Swan, and Todd (1976) examined salespersons' perceptions of their employer's management control system and job performance in the pharmaceutical industry. Futrell et al.'s research was the only research located in the literature that examined the relationship between sales management control and sales performance in the pharmaceutical industry. The sales management control constructs used in the study were different from the seminal work by Anderson and Oliver (1987) and Jaworski (1988). In Futrell et al.'s (1976) study, management control system was defined as the formal systems for setting objectives, measuring performance, and taking action in order to enhance performance; the management control system constructs for the study included goal clarity, performance-rewards relationship, influence and control impact, and job performance. The study sample included the total sales staff and their immediate supervisors in two national pharmaceutical companies and one national hospital-supply company.

The purpose of Futrell et al.'s (1976) study was to examine goal clarity, performance-reward relationships, and influence and control on job performance. The conceptual model hypothesized that higher performing salespeople, as compared to lower performing salespeople, would tend to have the following perceptions:

1. High clarity about the management control system

2. High personal influence and control over establishing job goals

3. Job rewards based on performance.

The results of a canonical correlation analysis reported that three constructs of the control system were significantly related to job performance, namely, goal clarity, performance-reward relationships, and influence and control (Futrell et al., 1976). However, the explanatory strengths of these relationships between the predictor and criterion variables were weak. According to Futrell et al., the canonical correlation analysis implied that 9% (clarity) to 17% (performance-rewards) of the variation in performance was explained by the control system variables.

Futrell et al.'s (1976) findings showed an association between salespersons' perceived control over their work situation and job performance. According to Futrell et al., the most likely reason for this association is the increase in perceived power and participative decision making, which create an increased commitment to attain job goals within the salesperson. Based on the findings, Futrell et al. recommended that organizations allow salespeople enough freedom to feel they have control over their sales jobs.

Futrell et al.'s (1976) study demonstrated that expected rewards have a strong relationship to performance. Anticipated benefits from the organization were related directly to willingness to work, a positive attitude, and performance improvement. Although compensation and other rewards have an important relationship to a salesperson's performance, the sales manager can also use the attributes of individual control and system clarity to influence a salesperson's performance.

Finally, Futrell et al. (1976) suggested that salespeople should have considerable control over the means of accomplishing the job goals for which they are held responsible. The goals and their importance need to be made clear to salespeople, and salespeople's supervisors should provide periodic feedback about job performance in relation to expectations. Rewards or penalties can be administered contingent upon meeting performance goals.

Sales Territory Design

Zoltners and Lorimer (2000) estimated that the majority of companies (80%) operating in the United States have imbalanced sales territory alignments that result in sales loses of 2% to 7%. According to Zoltners and Lorimer, when territories are out of balance, too much effort is deployed with low potential customers and too little effort is deployed with many high potential customers. The result is that companies often lose millions of dollars. Good territory design is important for several reasons. According to Zoltners and Lorimer, good sales territories enhance customer coverage, foster fair performance evaluation and reward systems, and lower travel costs. Experienced sales managers acknowledge that poor territory designs are likely to reduce salesperson performance and sales unit effectiveness (Piercy et al., 2004).

Despite the recognition of the potential financial impact of imbalanced territories, minimal research has examined the relationship amongst sales territory design, sales

66

performance, and sales organization effectiveness (Piercy et al., 2004). Considering the major role of selling activities in many organizations, the minimal amount of research about sales territory design is an oversight. According to Cravens et al. (1993), considering the high cost of a sales force and its influence on customer satisfaction, the lack of research on sales territory design is a significant gap in the sales force literature.

Companies use different factors to design sales territories (Babakus et al., 1996). The majority of sales territories include pre-assigned geography, customers, and accounts. According to Babakus et al., sales territories include a combination of all three in many cases. Prior research has emphasized the importance of sales territory design as a predictor of salesperson performance (Babakus et al., 1996; Cravens et al., 1992; Piercy et al., 1999).

The evidence from the research strongly supported the proposition that sales territory design can have a significant influence on the performance and effectiveness of sales organizations. Dickson (1994) recommended that sales territory design should be a precursor or prototype for developing effective corporate marketing structures at a broader level. Despite previous research findings that highlight the importance of sales territory design as a predictor of sales and organizational effectiveness, minimal empirical research exists about the topic (Piercy et al., 2004). Piercy et al. (1999) proffered that when sales territories are too large or small, salesperson efficiency and effectiveness are reduced. As a result, salesperson performance may be negatively affected. According to Piercy et al., sales territory design requires examination as one of the possible predictors of sales organization effectiveness.

The sales territory design construct is important to many sales organizations (Piercy et al., 1999). Sales managers within individual divisions of organizations consider the sales territory design construct when assessing efficiency and effectiveness of sales territory structure. The sales territory design construct is also employed when deciding on such actions as determining territory borders, the number of salespeople needed, and how to distribute salesperson effort across different customer segments.

Previous studies have examined sales force deployment and sales territory design constructs (Achrol, 1991; Beswick & Cravens, 1977; LaForge & Cravens, 1985; Lodish, 1980). According to Babakus et al. (1996), a significant amount of empirical evidence gathered from a large cross section of companies suggested that a suboptimal sales territory design could negate sales managements' efforts to improve salesperson performance. Empirical evidence also supports a link between effective sales territory design and salesperson performance (Cravens, Woodruff, & Stamper, 1972), implying that effective sales territory design decisions provide the opportunity for exceptional salesperson performance.

Many companies appear to operate with various sales territory design imbalances. Past research (Piercy et al., 1999) suggested that improving the balance in sales territory design could improve salesperson effectiveness. Empirical evidence implied that opportunities to improve the effectiveness of decisions regarding sales organization structure, sales force size, territory design, and allocation of selling effort exist (Beswick & Cravens, 1977; LaForge & Cravens, 1985; Lodish, 1974; Rangaswamy et al., 1990; Zoltners & Sinha, 1983). A significant amount of empirical evidence supported the need for improving sales territory design.

According to Piercy et al. (1999), sales managers who employ behavior-based control for salespeople will likely pay closer attention to sales territory design because the territory determines the scope and potential for the salesperson to undertake the behaviors desired. Empirical research by Piercy et al. and Babakus et al. (1996) showed that sales territory design significantly influenced the behavior-based and outcome-based performance of salespersons. Salespeople paid mainly by a fixed salary represent substantial investments, and their productivity is directly affected by the appropriateness and efficiency of sales territory design (Piercy et al., 1999).

In contrast, the use of outcome-based control means a high proportion of total salesperson salary is commission or bonus based; consequently, fixed costs are relatively low (Piercy et al., 1999). Under outcome-based control, managers appear less likely to emphasize territory design issues like territory boundaries and sales force size or allocation (Piercy et al., 1999). The primary focus in outcome-based control is generating sales volume or an equivalent commission-earning outcome measure.

Sales Force Performance

The distinction between sales organization effectiveness and sales force performance has received considerable empirical support (Beswick & Cravens, 1997; Cravens et al., 1972; LaForge & Cravens, 1985; Ryans & Weinberg, 1979, 1987). The support rests on the findings that variations in sales organization effectiveness may be explained by changes in environmental factors, such as competition, and organizational factors, such as management control systems, advertising spending, and brand image, as well as by salesperson factors. Sales organization effectiveness and salesperson performance are related but conceptually different constructs: *Sales organization effectiveness* is a summary evaluation of overall organizational outcomes (Babakus et al., 1996). According to Babakus et al., these outcomes can only be partly attributed to the salesperson.

Because organizational outcomes can only be partly attributed to the salesperson, evaluations of salesperson performance should be restricted to factors under the control of salespeople (Babakus et al., 1996). Assessments of sales organization effectiveness are overall results determined by many situational factors including salesperson performance (Piercy et al., 1999). The performance of salespeople contributes to but does not completely determine sales organization effectiveness. According to Challagalla and Shervani (1996), the effects of a single variable on performance such as a control system alone may be misleading; performance will also be affected by other variables.

In addition, several studies (Babakus et al., 1996; Cravens et al., 1993; Oliver & Anderson, 1994; Piercy et al., 2004) divided the salesperson performance construct into a behavioral performance dimension and an outcome performance dimension. Because salespeople can more directly control what they do, behavioral performance measures have been proposed and used in a number of studies (Babakus et al., 1996; Cravens et al., 1993; Jaworski & Kohli, 1991; MacKinzie, Podkasoff, & Fetter, 1993; Piercy et al., 2004; Walker et al., 1979). However, while the behavioral aspects of performance are important, salespeople also produce outcomes largely attributed to them, representing an outcome performance dimension. Outcome performance is a separate component of performance, both conceptually (Anderson & Oliver, 1987; Walker et al., 1979) and empirically (Behrman & Perreault, 1982, 1984; Challagalla & Shervani, 1996; Cravens et al., 1993; Jaworski & Kohli, 1991; Oliver & Anderson, 1994).

A significant amount of research maintained that salesperson performance comprises components of both behavior-based and outcome-based performance constructs (Babakus et al., 1996). Behavior-based performance comprises an assessment of how well salespeople execute their required sales activities and strategies to attract and retain customers. Managing within a behavior-based management structure requires sales managers to assess performance by focusing on the daily inputs of their salespeople, such as number of sales calls and strategy implementation, rather than on outputs, such as sales results. An example of behavior-based performance is customer support and planning by salespeople (Anderson & Oliver, 1987). Other elements of behavior-based performance include teamwork, delivering sales presentations, product and technical knowledge, and adaptive selling.

The results achieved from salespeople's efforts and skills comprise the salesperson outcome-based performance. Babakus et al. (1996) indicated that typical outcome performance measures include market share, product sales volume, and customer acquisition and retention. Organizations practicing behavior-based management control achieve a higher level of behavior-based performance, resulting in improved organization outcome-based performance (Babakus et al., 1996).

Cravens et al. (1993) provided empirical support that a positive relationship exists among behavior-based, outcome-based, and sales organization effectiveness. Piercy et al.'s (1998) research results suggested that substantial differences exist between those sales units with high and low outcome performance for behavior-based salesperson performance components, including sales planning, product and technical knowledge, teamwork, adaptive selling, and customer service. Salespeople with higher behavior-based performance achieved higher outcome performance. Substantial variation in behavior-based and outcome-based performance is predicted for high performing sales teams as compared to low performing sales teams.

Sales Organization Effectiveness

An increasing amount of research has focused on the influence of sales performance on sales organization effectiveness. Walker et al. (1979) explained sales organization effectiveness as a composite of organization results for which the salesperson is in some measure responsible. Key indicators of sales organization performance include market share, sales volume, and profitability.

Each sales division contributes to the achievement of sales organization effectiveness. These sales divisions consist of a number of smaller sales units managed by a sales manager (Babakus et al., 1996; Cravens et al., 1993; Churchill et al., 1997; Piercy et al., 2004). The smaller units within the sales division are called districts, regions, or customer segments (Babakus et al., 1996; Cravens et al., 1993; Churchill et al., 1997). The salespeople employed within the smaller units are responsible for acquiring and retaining customers (Babakus et al., 1996). According to Babakus et al., their performance is critical to sales organization effectiveness.

Past research in personal selling hinted at a relationship between salesperson performance and sales organization effectiveness (Babakus et al., 1996; Cravens et al., 1993; Churchill et al., 1997). According to Churchill et al. (1985), prior research that attempted to discover the factors influencing salesperson effectiveness has been unsuccessful. However, minimal research was focused on understanding the possible factors associated with sales unit effectiveness. According to Churchill et al. (1997), a key determinant of sales unit effectiveness, the sales manager, has received minimal research attention. Emphasis in prior research on salesperson performance may have concealed the role the sales manager plays in affecting sales unit effectiveness.

Babakus et al. (1996) described sales organization effectiveness as a component of total organizational outcomes. Sales organization effectiveness can be measured and observed for the entire sales organization or for individual sales units within divisions of the sales organization (Babakus et al., 1996). According to Babakus et al., individual divisions will employ smaller sales units led by a sales manager. The performance measurements often used to determine sales organization effectiveness for individual divisions and the overall organization includes the evaluation of total sales, cost of sales, profit margin and contribution, and return on assets. A number of researchers (Churchill et al., 1997; Cron & Levy, 1987; Dubinsky & Barry, 1982; Jackson, Keith, & Schlacter, 1983; LaForge, 1992; Morris, Davis, Allen, Avila, & Chapman, 1991) have recognized performance measures such as sales organization effectiveness. Babakus et al. (1996) identified customer satisfaction as another important dimension of sales organization effectiveness.

An important finding from previous research (Babakus et al., 1996) is that the salesperson is not the only influence on sales unit effectiveness. According to Babakus et al., multiple factors explain the variance in salesperson performance. These factors may include inadequate organizational policies, external market dynamics, and poor sales management practices. Despite these findings, many sales organizations criticize the salesperson when sales unit performance is below expectations. Sales organizations are perceived to place unreasonable performance expectations on their salespeople. Based on research by Babakus et al., it is critical for management to consider both the controllable and uncontrollable factors when devising sales goals for salespeople.

Conclusion

The foregoing discussion demonstrates that much of the previous research in the sales management field has focused on understanding and improving sales organization performance by assessing the characteristics of individual salesperson's performance. These studies have not offered an explanation about what influences overall sales organization performance and effectiveness (Churchill et al., 1985; Mount & Barrick, 1995; Vinchur et al., 1998). Research studies that have focused on the importance of situational contingencies such as systems of sales management control and territory design choices have increased (Grant & Cravens, 1996). Past research has established that situational contingencies such as systems of sales management control may act as moderators and/or predictors of sales force performance (Babakus et al., 1996; Cravens et al., 1993; Darmon, 1993; Ganesan et al., 1993; Grant & Cravens, 1996; Oliver & Anderson, 1994; Piercy et al., 1999; Weitz et al., 1986). The analysis of such contingencies is apparent in research that focuses on sales management practices and sales organizations rather than the characteristics of individual salespeople. Understanding these relationships within sales organizations in the pharmaceutical industry may provide pharmaceutical sales management with information to improve sales organization effectiveness.

While sales force deployment and sale territory design approaches have been examined in previous studies (Achrol, 1991; Beswick & Cravens, 1977; Day, 1997; LaForge & Cravens, 1985; Lodish, 1980; Piercy, 1985; Piercy & Cravens, 1995;

Webster, 1992), in these studies, sales territory design has not been associated with outcome performance. In addition, according to Babakus et al. (1996), limited research has been conducted about the interaction between sales management activities and sales territory design issues. Recognizing the significant role of salespeople in many organizations, high cost of the sales function, profound effects of the sales force on customer retention and satisfaction, and sales forces' influence on the profitability of the firm, the limited investment in research about sales territory design appears to be an oversight (Babakus et al., 1996).

Given increasing competitive pressure, increasing pressures to control costs, and the rising costs of sales, understanding the predictors of sales organization effectiveness is critical to sales organizations within the pharmaceutical industry (Seget, 2004). At the time of the literature review, one study (Futrell et al., 1976) had examined the influence of sales management control on salesperson performance in the pharmaceutical industry. The constructs used in the study were different from those identified in the seminal management control research by Anderson and Oliver (1987). The results of the study suggested a weak relationship between sales management control and salesperson performance (Futrell et al., 1976).

Minimal empirical research within sales organizations in the pharmaceutical industry is a major limitation in the body of literature about sales management control. The limitation is important, particularly considering the major role that selling activities play in many pharmaceutical organizations and the correspondingly high cost of the sales function. To address the limitation, the present study tested constructs associated with sales management control (Babakus et al., 1996) in a sales organization within the pharmaceutical industry.

Summary

Sales management research about improving sales organization performance and effectiveness has been focused on identifying the characteristics of individual salesperson performance. According to Churchill et al. (1985), these studies have produced inconsistent results with respect to the factors affecting sales organization performance. In addition, the hypothesized predictors explained little of the variation in salesperson performance (Churchill et al., 1995; Mount & Barrick, 1995; Vinchur et al., 1998). In a meta-analysis of the factors affecting salesperson performance, Churchill et al. (1985) found no single salesperson characteristic that could explain the significant variation in sales performance amongst sales representatives and concluded that no single factor or even several factors in a single category of predictors could accurately predict salespeople's future sales performance. In addition, theoretical models that hypothesize multiple determinants and categories of determinants of salesperson performance were more accurate for explaining sales performance. Whether the shortfalls found in the meta-analysis by Churchill et al. represent attention to the incorrect sales performance indicators and sales performance dimensions or merely the use of poor sales performance measures is still uncertain (Piercy et al., 1996).

The theoretical and empirical studies reviewed offered other approaches to improving sales force performance. The findings from these studies (Babakus et al., 1996; Cravens et al., 1993; Piercy et al., 1999; Piercy et al., 2004) proposed that improving sales force performance requires increased emphasis on assessing salesperson job behavior, as opposed to only salesperson results. Salesperson performance in activities such as the number of sales calls, preparing for sales calls, presenting sales information, and the degree of participation in team-based selling might be a substantial contributor to overall sales organization effectiveness (Piercy et al., 1999).

Researchers and sales executives recognize the importance of situational contingencies such as systems of sales management control and sales territory design (Babakus et al., 1996). These contingencies may act as moderators and/or predictors of sales organization effectiveness. The analysis of such contingencies is apparent in research focused on sales management practices and sales organizations as opposed to the characteristics of individual salespeople. Prior research studies (Babakus et al., 1996; Cravens et al., 1993; Darmon, 1993; Ganesan et al., 1993; Grant & Cravens, 1996; Oliver & Anderson, 1994; Piercy et al., 1999; Piercy et al., 2004; Weitz et al., 1986) supported the seminal work by Anderson and Oliver (1987) that a positive relationship exists between behavior-based performance and the affective and motivational states of salespeople. However, the strength of the relationship between the factors and sales organization performance were weak. Few of these studies (Babakus et al., 1996; Cravens et al., 1993; Darmon, 1993; Ganesan et al., 1993; Grant & Cravens, 1996; Oliver & Anderson, 1994; Piercy et al., 1999; Piercy et al., 2004; Weitz et al., 1986) examined these relationships within sales organization in the pharmaceutical industry.

When evaluating sales force performance, the sales manager should separate and recognize uncontrollable factors that can influence individual salesperson's outcome performance such as market potential (Piercy et al., 1996). Both controllable and uncontrollable factors are significant for understanding what drives sales performance.

Both controllable and uncontrollable factors require consideration when selecting measures of sales management control.

Wide support exists for effective sales territory design (Babakus et al., 1996; Piercy, 1985). Dickson (1994) recommended that sales territory design should be a precursor or prototype for developing effective corporate marketing structures at a broader level. According to Babakus et al. (1996), empirical evidence indicated that suboptimal territory design negatively influenced sales managements' efforts to improve the outcome of sales force performance.

Distinguishing between sales organization effectiveness and sales force performance has been validated empirically (Beswick & Cravens, 1997; Cravens et al., 1972; LaForge & Cravens, 1985; Ryans & Weinberg, 1979, 1987). Research found that variations in sales organization effectiveness are explained by changes in environmental factors such as competition; organizational factors such as management control systems, advertising spending, and brand image; and salesperson factors such as sales activities (Piercy et al., 1999). These studies noted that sales organization effectiveness and sales force performance are related but conceptually different constructs. Sales organization effectiveness is a summary evaluation of organizational outcomes (Babakus et al., 1996). According to Babakus et al. (1996), the salesperson is only partially responsible for these outcomes.

Whether considered through agency theory or transaction cost analysis, circumstances under which a firm should select an outcome-based or behavior-based philosophy of sales management control can be identified. Anderson and Oliver (1987) proposed that systems of sales management control be positioned somewhere on a continuum ranging from purely behavior-based to purely outcome-based. An outcome-based system of sales management control monitors the final outputs, such as sales or profits, and requires minimal salesperson supervision, simple performance measures, and compensation plans such as commission plans. Behavior-based systems of sales management control evaluate salesperson behavior and activities on such actions as customer service and sales call planning.

The study findings by Babakus et al. (1996) indicated that systems of sales management control are strongly related to both sales territory design and behavioral performance. In addition, behavior performance is a significant factor of outcome performance. Based on the results of Babakus et al.'s research, understanding these relationships in sales organizations within the pharmaceutical industry may provide pharmaceutical sales management with information to improve sales organization effectiveness. The details of how these relationships were explored in the present study are discussed in chapter 3.

CHAPTER 3: METHOD

The purpose of the present study is to examine the relationships between sales management control, sales territory design, sales force performance, and sales organization effectiveness in sales organizations within the pharmaceutical industry. Past research results from different industries suggested that examining situational contingencies such as sales management control and sales territory design may provide an alternative approach for identifying factors to improve sales organization effectiveness (Grant & Cravens, 1996). Figure 2 illustrates the empirical model for the present study. The figure shows the independent variables, namely, sales management control, sales force performance, behavioral and outcome performance, and sales territory design. The figure also shows the dependent variable, namely, sales organization effectiveness and hypothesized relationships between the constructs. The present study used the empirical model to test hypotheses among sales managers in a sales organization in the pharmaceutical industry. The remainder of chapter 3 will describe the main components of the research method used.

Research Design

A quantitative research methodology using an explanatory correlation research design was employed. In correlation research designs, a correlation technique is used to describe and measure the degree of association or relationship between two or more variables or sets of scores (Creswell, 2002). A correlation research design does not attempt to control or manipulate variables. Instead, the design is used to relate two or more scores using the correlation coefficient. Creswell identified two primary forms of correlation research: explanation and prediction. Correlation research assists with

explaining the association between two or more variables or predicts an outcome.

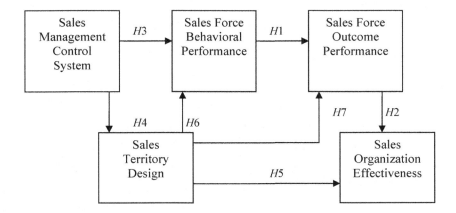

Figure 2. Empirical model used for the proposed study.

From "Investigating the relationships among sales management control, sales territory design, salesperson

performance, and sales organizational effectiveness," by E. Babakus, D. W. Cravens, K. Grant, T. N.

Ingram, and R. W. LaForge, 1996, *International Journal of Research in Marketing, 13*(4), p. 353.

Copyright 1996 by Elsevier Publishing. Reprinted with permission of the author.

Based on the purpose of the present study, employing a quantitative explanatory

correlation research design is considered appropriate. The purpose of the present study is

to explain the magnitude of the relationships between the independent variables of sales

management control, sales territory design, and sales force performance and the

dependent variable of sales organizational effectiveness within sales organizations in the

pharmaceutical industry.

Appropriateness of Design

In a quantitative research methodology, problems in which trends need to be described or explanations developed for relationships between variables are studied (Creswell, 2002). In contrast, qualitative research is used to examine a research problem in which a central phenomenon is explored. According to Creswell, an exploration implies that little is known about the phenomenon under investigation and more needs to be learned from the participants. Because the present study is an extension of prior quantitative research and endeavors to explain the relationship between variables, using a quantitative explanatory correlation research design is considered appropriate.

Quantitative research can be divided into intervention and nonintervention research (Creswell, 2002). Intervention research, such as experimental and quasi-experimental research, is used to explain whether an intervention influences an outcome for one group as opposed to another group. Nonintervention research, such as correlation research, is focused on examining the association or relationship among one or more variables. Consistent with nonintervention research, the present study examined the relationships among variables using a correlation research design.

Research Question

The present study was designed to answer the following research question:

R1: What relationships exist between sales management control, sales territory design, sales force performance, and sales organization effectiveness in the pharmaceutical industry?

Hypotheses

The following null hypotheses were evaluated using data collected from a sample of district managers employed by Octagon Pharmaceutical, located in the northeastern part of the United States.

$H1_0$: No significant correlation exists between the level of sales force behavioral

performance and the level of sales force outcome performance.

$H2_0$: No significant correlation exists between the level of sales force outcome

performance and the level of sales organization effectiveness.

$H3_0$: No significant correlation exists between the extent of behavior-based sales

management control and the level of sales force behavioral performance.

$H4_0$: No significant correlation exists between the extent of behavior-based sales

management control and the level of satisfaction with sales territory design.

$H5_0$: No significant correlation exists between the extent of satisfaction with sales

territory design and the level of sales organization effectiveness.

$H6_0$: No significant correlation exists between the extent of satisfaction with sales

territory design and the level of sales force behavioral performance.

$H7_0$: No significant correlation exists between the extent of satisfaction with sales

territory design and the level of sales force outcome performance.

Population

The population for the present study consisted of district managers in a sales organization within the pharmaceutical industry. According to Curry and Frost (2001), district managers in pharmaceutical sales organizations are responsible for managing territory sales representatives within a specific locale. Pharmaceutical sales organization's structures are multilevel, and within those structures, the district manager is considered the midlevel sales manager. The field sales unit supervised by district managers was the unit of analysis. Consistent with previous research, which examined sales management control constructs (Babakus et al., 1996; Piercy et al., 1999), the district manager was selected as the appropriate information source for the study unit of analysis because the conceptual model tested for the present study incorporates organizational variables not easily evaluated by salespeople (Baldauf et al., 2000).

The district managers were asked to evaluate their own activities and those of their field sales unit. The field sales unit typically comprises a group of salespeople reporting to a first-line field sales manager and is a common denominator across sales organizations (Piercy et al., 1999). Unlike previous studies that were focused on sales management control, the present study does not focus on addressing issues related to the number of levels or the structuring of the broader sales organization, but is limited to a focus on the field sales unit in a sales organization within the pharmaceutical industry.

District managers in the pharmaceutical industry are responsible for managing a sales district. A typical sales district has 8–12 territory sales representatives (Curry & Frost, 2001). Each territory sales representative within the sales district has responsibility for generating sales from a specific sales territory. According to Curry and Frost, territory sales representatives are responsible for developing profitable relationships with assigned customers, including physicians and office staff. Territory sales representatives interact with these customers in individual and/or group practice settings.

The district manager's primary responsibility is to supervise, guide, coach, and develop territory sales representatives (Curry & Frost, 2001). The outcomes expected from these actions are the achievement of pre-assigned goals for the territory sales representative such as calls per day, presentations per day, and resource allocation. District managers are responsible for ensuring their territory sales representatives achieve the required behaviors and outcomes.

Curry and Frost (2001) suggested that district managers contact their territory sales representatives on a regular basis to coach and direct their activities. District manager coaching occurs primarily during scheduled work sessions with territory sales representatives. The work sessions consist of the district manager accompanying the representative in the field during sales calls to observe and provide feedback about their selling interaction with customers. The district manager reinforces appropriate selling behavior and seeks to discourage and improve inappropriate selling behavior. According to Curry and Frost, the district manager is also required to train new and tenured territory sales representatives and facilitate quarterly district sales meetings.

Sampling Frame

Creswell (2002) defined a sample as a subgroup of the larger population that is the focus of a study. According to Creswell, the purpose of using a sample is to generalize the research results to the target population. The target population for the present study is district managers employed by different operating companies within Octagon Pharmaceutical located in the northeastern part of the United States. Octagon Pharmaceutical consists of four separate pharmaceutical operating companies with different customer and product portfolios. Each operating company has different sales management personnel. The objective of the sampling plan is to include district managers from each of the operating companies within Octagon Pharmaceutical. District managers

85

sampled for the present study varied by operating company, performance, industry tenure, and district manager experience.

According to Creswell (2002), the most rigorous form of sampling in quantitative research is probability sampling. In probability sampling, individuals are selected from a target population that is representative of the total population being studied. According to Creswell, probability sampling is the most rigorous form of sampling in quantitative research because a claim that the sample is representative of the population studied can be made and, as such, generalizations to the population can be made. A less rigorous form of sampling is called non-probability sampling where individuals are selected because they are available and convenient and represent some characteristic the investigator seeks to study (Creswell, 2002). Probability sampling is used for the present study.

According to Creswell, the intent of simple random sampling is to choose units that will be representative of the target population. The sampling approach used for the present study was simple random sampling. The target population for the present study was district managers within Octagon Pharmaceutical. Senior management of Octagon Pharmaceutical provided a list of 400 district managers to participate in the present study. The sample for the present study was chosen from the list of 400 district managers using simple random sampling so that the findings of the study could be generalized to the target population. A random numbers table was used to select the individuals for the study sample.

Sample Size

When selecting participants for a study, determining the size of the sample is essential. Creswell (2002) maintained that a general rule is to select as large a sample as possible from the population or from the individuals available. The larger the sample, the more similar it will be to the population and the more dependable generalizations made will be. One way to determine the sample size is to select a sufficient number of participants for the statistical procedures that will be used (Creswell, 2002). As a rough estimate, Creswell suggested the following:

1. the selection of approximately 15 participants in each group in an experiment,

2. the selection of approximately 30 participants for a correlation study to relate variables, and

3. the selection of approximately 350 individuals for a survey study (Creswell, 2002).

These numbers are estimates based on the size needed for statistical procedures such as group comparisons, relating variables, and obtaining a large enough sample in a survey so that the findings based on the sample are likely to be reliable estimates of the characteristics of the population (Creswell, 2002).

The sample size goal for the present study is large enough to relate variables. The sample plan for the present quantitative explanatory correlation study called for a sample of 100 district managers. The district managers' performances varied from high to average to low as indicated by the most recent company annual sales performance ranking. The district managers were employed within four separate sales organizations at Octagon Pharmaceutical.

Informed Consent

Permission was granted from the senior management of Octagon Pharmaceutical (see Appendix A) to collect data from the company's district managers. Octagon Pharmaceutical financed the research and necessary coursework with the agreement that the doctoral research be conducted in the organization and the results shared with the organization. Senior management of Octagon Pharmaceutical notified district managers (see Appendix B) and asked them to volunteer to participate in the study. Participants were required to acknowledge consent of voluntary participation by signing the Informed Consent Form (see Appendix C) before completing the research questionnaire.

Confidentiality

Permission was obtained from senior management of Octagon Pharmaceutical to collect data from district managers. Participant responses were kept anonymous and confidential. The results of the study will be reported to the senior management of Octagon Pharmaceutical as part of the conditions for conducting the study, as well as be submitted as part of the doctoral dissertation requirements to the University of Phoenix.

To ensure confidentiality of participants' responses, all data was coded using a numerical prefix. The list of numerical prefixes or codes was secured in a locked cabinet. Only the researcher could access the contents of the cabinet. All data will be destroyed after three years in order to avoid access or its reconstruction.

Geographic Location

The sample of district managers who participated in the study were employed by Octagon Pharmaceutical and resided in different locations in the United States.

Data Collection

Data was collected in a manner consistent with previous sales management control research (Babakus et al., 1996; Piercy et al., 1999). The sample for the present study was district managers employed by Octagon Pharmaceutical who resided in different locations in the United States. Data was collected using an electronic questionnaire completed by district managers in the participating organization; the field sales unit was the unit of analysis. District managers evaluated their field sales unit by answering questions on the administered questionnaire. Participants accessed the electronic questionnaire via the Internet.

The research questionnaire was emailed to the study participants with specific directions for completion. A high response rate was expected because the study sample was notified and asked to volunteer to complete the questionnaire by senior management at Octagon Pharmaceutical. According to Creswell (2002), using the electronic questionnaire reduces the risk of inaccurate data collection from the study participants and increases the probability of accurate responses and timely completion of the questionnaire.

Instrumentation

The instrument used was a questionnaire (see Appendix D). The questionnaire was consistent with previous research from other industries conducted in the United States, Canada, Australia, Greece, India, Malaysia, and the United Kingdom (Babakus et al., 1996; Cravens et al., 1993; Grant & Cravens, 1996; Piercy et al., 1999) and was designed to test the hypotheses developed for the study. The instrument and scales used have been validated in earlier studies (Babakus et al., 1996; Piercy et al., 1999); consequently, no need to pretest the instrument before administering it was deemed necessary.

The questionnaire was used to collect data for the independent variables of sales management control, sales territory design, and sales force performance and the dependent variable, sales organization effectiveness. The data collected was consistent with previous studies (Babakus et al., 1996; Cravens et al., 1993; Grant & Cravens, 1996; Piercy et al., 1999; Piercy et al., 2004) that investigated the relationships between sales management control, sales territory design, sales force performance, and sales organizational effectiveness in different target populations. Consistent with past research (Babakus et al., 1996; Piercy et al., 1999) district managers evaluated their field sales unit regarding the relationships between the independent and dependent variables by answering questions from the administered questionnaire.

In order to collect data on each variable, how to measure, observe, and document the variable must be defined (Creswell, 2002). Given that the present study extended previous research, the same constructs and measurements of the constructs from the previous research was used to study a new sample. Consistent with previous sales management control research (Babakus et al., 1996; Piercy et al., 1999; Piercy et al., 2004) the construct measures in the present study were treated as continuous scales. Each of the constructs measured are listed and defined below:

Systems of sales management control. The extent to which sales management control is behavior-based is evaluated by a series of questions measuring the extent of sales manager monitoring, guiding, assessing, and compensating salespeople. The extent of these actions was measured on a 10-point scale. The 10-point scale is anchored by the options to a great extent and not at all. The sales management control construct was measured using a scale based on previous research (Anderson & Oliver, 1987; Babakus et al., 1996).

Sales territory design. The sales territory design construct was measured using a multiple-item scale developed by Babakus et al. (1996). The participants were asked to indicate their level of satisfaction with the design of sales territories in their sales district. A 7-point scale was used. The 7-point scale is anchored by the descriptors very satisfied and not at all satisfied. The measurement of the construct of sales territory design does not consider all possible aspects of territory and field sales unit design (Babakus et al., 1996).

Sales force performance. Researchers have separated sales force performance into two dimensions: (a) the behavior or activities performed by salespeople, and (b) the outcomes or results attained through salespeople's efforts (Anderson & Oliver, 1987; Cravens et al., 1993). The two dimensions are designated as behavior-based and outcome-based performance (Anderson & Oliver, 1987; Behrmann & Perreault, 1982). Sales force performance included the measurement of both dimensions and was measured using a modified and extended form of the multiple-item scale developed by Behrmann and Perreault (1982, 1984). A 7-point scale was used and was anchored with the terms outstanding and needs improvement. Sales force outcome performance was assessed using a multiple-item scale developed by Babakus et al. (1996). The multiple-item scale assessed achievements in outcome performance measures of market share, sales, and profitability.

Sales organization effectiveness. Previous research (Babakus et al., 1996; Cravens et al., 1993; Grant & Cravens, 1996; Piercy et al., 1999) measured sales organization effectiveness as a summary rating of sales, market share, profitability, and customer satisfaction achievements compared to the major competitors and compared to sales unit objectives. The same strategy was adopted for this research: Eight items, each measured by a 5-point scale, measured sales organization effectiveness. The 5-point scale was anchored by the descriptors much worse and much better than the competition. Cravens et al. (1993) developed the 5-point scale.

Reliability

According to Creswell (2002), reliability means that individual scores from an instrument should be nearly the same or stable on repeated administration of the instrument. Previous research about sales management control (Babakus et al., 1996; Piercy et al., 1999; Piercy et al., 2004) provided evidence of the reliability of the questionnaire used for the present study. Data collected by Babakus et al. (1996) for the items comprising each dimension were analyzed to examine reliability. Babakus et al. performed an exploratory factor analysis on the same set of items used in the present study.

The purpose of the exploratory factor analysis was to establish whether the items represented the distinct concepts of interest (Babakus et al., 1996). Analysis using Cronbach's alpha coefficient (Cronbach, 1970) and correlation analysis were used to further refine the measures and eliminate items whose inclusion resulted in lower alpha coefficients (Babakus et al., 1996). Table 2 presents the correlations among the measures and Cronbach's alpha coefficients for each measure in the study (Babakus et al., 1996). The scale reliabilities, coefficient alpha, are on the diagonal. An inspection of the alpha coefficients in Table 2 reveal that all coefficients were greater than .70, and 11 of the 15 multiple-item measures had coefficients greater than .80 (Babakus et al., 1996). According to Nunnally (1978), coefficients greater than .70 indicate good test-retest reliability.

Subsequent research (Piercy et al., 1999) employed the questionnaire used by Babakus et al. (1996). The alpha coefficients are all above .76 with 11 of the 13 multiple-item measures displaying coefficients greater than .80 (Piercy et al., 1999). The present study employed the same research questionnaire used by Babakus et al. (1996) and Piercy et al. (1999). Based on the reliability results from these studies (Babakus et al., 1996; Piercy et al., 1999) and the subsequent results from research using the same questionnaire (Piercy et al., 2004), the questionnaire used for the present study has an adequate level of reliability.

Validity: Internal and External

Validity means that meaningful and justifiable inferences can be drawn from scores in a sample or population (Creswell, 2002). Evaluating a valid instrument for a study requires assessing whether scores from the previous use of the instrument are valid and useful: "When reviewing instruments for use in a study, consider whether the authors report validity for scores from its use" (Creswell, 2002, p. 183). The scores from the instrument and scales used for the present study have been reported and have been

Table 2.

Correlations and Reliability Estimates (N = 146)

Measures	1	2	3	4	5	6	7	8	9	10	11	12	13	14	15
Design															
Y_1	0.88														
Behavioral performance															
Y_2	0.146	0.84													
Y_3	0.281	0.491	0.91												
Y_4	0.290	0.303	0.448	0.78											
Y_5	0.280	0.508	0.689	0.445	0.085										
Y_6	0.289	0.334	0.553	0.335	0.612	0.89									
Y_7	0.112	0.380	0.389	0.457	0.563	0.467	0.86								
Outcome performance															
Y8	0.399	0.449	0.557	0.308	0.561	0.576	0.310	0.84							
Effectiveness															
Y_9	0.288	0.231	0.228	0.026	0.127	0.200	-0.035	0.482	0.88						
Y_{10}	0.273	0.243	0.170	0.147	0.109	0.049	-0.054	0.292	0.391	0.77					
Y_{11}	0.283	0.344	0.351	0.164	0.375	0.230	0.234	0.213	0.361	0.338	0.81				
Activities															
X_1	0.284	0.195	0.291	0.029	0.262	0.282	0.160	0.329	0.193	0.071	-0.021	0.79			
X_2	0.249	0.088	0.201	0.030	0.154	0.122	-0.009	0.221	0.081	0.223	-0.002	0.636	0.83		
X_3	0.299	0.211	0.230	0.131	0.224	0.198	0.199	0.364	0.175	0.229	-0.009	0.744	0.678	0.79	
X_4	0.190	0.147	0.131	0.097	0.081	0.124	0.003	0.241	0.071	0.166	0.009	0.531	0.598	0.60	0.86
$\bar{X}$	4.61	5.36	5.06	4.68	5.13	4.78	4.92	4.97	3.61	3.71	3.97	6.66	7.05	6.92	6.02
s	0.92	1.08	1.08	1.06	0.92	1.10	1.00	0.91	0.87	0.92	0.77	1.48	1.45	1.61	1.85

Note: Scale reliabilities (coefficient alpha) are on the diagonal. From "Investigating the relationships among sales management control, sales territory design, salesperson performance, and sales organizational effectiveness," by E. Babakus, D. W. Cravens, K. Grant, T. N. Ingram, and R. W. LaForge, 1996, *International Journal of Research in Marketing, 13*(4), p. 353. Copyright 1996 by Elsevier Publishing. Reprinted with permission of the author.

validated in earlier studies (Babakus et al., 1996; Cravens et al., 1993; Piercy et al., 1999; Piercy et al., 2004). The instrument for the present study was not pre-tested before administration due to prior validation of the research instrument and the scales.

Internal Validity

According to Creswell (2002), threats to internal validity are problems that threaten drawing correct inferences that arise because of the experimental procedure or the experience of participants. The instrument and scales for the present study have demonstrated internal validity in prior studies (Babakus et al., 1996; Piercy et al., 1999; Piercy et al., 2004). The research methodology and procedures for the present study was consistent with past research but in a different sample. The results from past studies suggested that the instrument and scales used for the present study will provide internal validity.

External Validity

According to Creswell (2002), threats to external validity are problems that threaten drawing correct inferences from sample data to other persons, settings, and past and future situations. The instrument and scales for the present study have demonstrated external validity in prior studies (Babakus et al., 1996; Piercy et al., 1999; Piercy et al., 2004). The scores from prior studies have enabled past researchers about the research topic to draw valid and justifiable inferences. The results from prior studies suggest that the instrument and scales used for the present study will provide external validity.

Content and Construct Validity

Bohrnstedt (1983) posited that validity is concerned with the question, "Did the test measure what it is intended to measure" (p. 135). According to Nunnally (1978), validity in a research study requires content validity, predictive validity, and construct validity. *Content validity* measures how well the questions represent all of the possible questions available, and *predictive validity* measures how well the scores on the instrument predict a future outcome. *Construct validity* provides an explanation for what scores on the instrument mean or signify (Creswell, 2002).

The instrument and scales for the present study have demonstrated content validity, predictive validity, and construct validity in past studies (Babakus et al., 1996; Piercy et al., 1999). Scores from past implementations of the instrument and scales used yielded accurate and reliable information and valid and justifiable inferences. According to Creswell (2002), past studies yielding accurate and reliable information and valid and justifiable inferences confirm the validity, internal and external, of a research instrument. Estimates of validity of the constructs and indicators in the present study were obtained using LISREL 8.80 (Jöreskog & Sörbom, 2006).

Data Analysis

The sequence of analysis involved in the present study included four stages. Stage 1 included a pre-analysis data examination and data preparation. Stage 2 included validation of the measures. Stage 3 included a correlation analysis of the constructs as guided by the hypotheses. Stage 4 included an assessment of the structural model and the path estimates. The hypotheses (see Table 3) listed earlier were tested and analyzed in the present study using AMOS 6.0. AMOS 6.0 (Arbuckle, 2005) is statistical software for correlation analysis and structure equation modeling. The chosen analytical approach is consistent with past research about sales management control (Babakus et al., 1996; Piercy et al., 1999; Piercy et al., 2004), which the present study extends to a new sample. The present study includes multiple independent variables. According to Creswell (2002), multiple regressions, or multiple correlations, are correlation statistical procedures for

96

Table 3.

Summary of Variables and Hypothesis Analysis

Research question and hypotheses	Source of data (variables)	Test statistic
RQ1: What relationships exist amongst sales management control, sales territory design, sales force performance, and sales organization effectiveness in the pharmaceutical industry?	Results of null hypotheses $H1$ through $H7$ answers research question	Multiple R
$H1$: No significant direct correlation exists between a higher level of sales force behavioral performance and a higher level of sales force outcome performance.	Sales force behavioral performance and sales force outcome performance survey questions	Multiple R
$H2$: No significant correlation exists between a higher level of salesperson outcome performance and a higher level of sales organization effectiveness.	Sales force outcome performance and sales organization effectiveness survey questions	Multiple R

Table 3. (continued)

Research question and hypotheses	Source of data (variables)	Test statistic
*H*3: No significant correlation exists between the extent of behavior-based sales management control and a higher level of salesperson behavioral performance.	Behavioral-based sales management control and sales force behavioral outcome performance survey questions	Multiple *R*
*H*4: No significant correlation exists between the extent of behavior-based sales management control and a higher level of satisfaction with sales territory design.	Behavioral-based sales management control and sales territory design survey questions	Multiple *R*
*H*5: No significant correlation exists between the extent of satisfaction with sales territory design and a higher level of sales organization effectiveness.	Sales territory design and sales organization effectiveness survey questions	Multiple *R*
*H*6: No significant correlation exists between the extent of satisfaction with the sales territory design and a higher level of sales force behavioral performance.	Sales territory design and sales force behavioral performance survey questions	Multiple *R*

Table 3. (continued)

Research question and hypotheses	Source of data (variables)	Test statistic
H7: There is no significant correlation between the extent of satisfaction with the sales territory design and a higher level of sales force outcome performance.	Sales territory design and sales force outcome performance survey questions	Multiple R

examining the combined relationship of multiple independent variables with a single dependent variable. In regression, the variation in the dependent variable is explained by the variance of each independent variable, as well as the combined effect of all independent variables designated R^2 (Kline, 1998). The present study used multiple regression coefficients to explain the influence of the independent variables of sales management control, sales territory design, and sales force performance on the dependent variable of sales organization effectiveness.

The aim of the research is to show how the predictor variables explain the association in the outcome variable in a visual model called a structural equation model. The structural equation model is a statistical procedure for testing a theory about a correlation sequence of three or more variables on an outcome variable (Creswell, 2002). AMOS 6.0 (Arbuckle, 2005) software was used to conduct the structural equation model analysis for the present study. Using multiple regressions, the weight of each predictor variable was determined with all other variables in the model held constant (Creswell, 2002). After completing multiple regressions, an assessment was made with respect to the combined contribution of each independent variable as well as each variable's individual contribution when controlling for other variables in the model.

Summary

The purpose of the present quantitative explanatory correlation study is to examine relationships between sales management control, sales territory design, sales force performance, and sales organization effectiveness in sales organizations with the pharmaceutical industry. The constructs for the present study extended previous research about sales management control (Babakus et al., 1996; Piercy et al., 1999; Piercy et al., 2004) to a new target population. Past research about sales management control has not been performed for sales organizations in the pharmaceutical industry.

The target population for the present study is district managers within the pharmaceutical industry. District managers have the responsibility to monitor, coach, and assess territory sales representatives' job activities and ensure that they achieve their assigned territory sales goals (Curry & Frost, 2001). The unit of analysis was the field sales unit, which typically comprises a group of salespeople reporting to a district manager. District managers evaluated their field sales unit regarding the relationships between the study independent and dependent variables by completing an electronic questionnaire. The sample of district managers came from four operating companies within Octagon Pharmaceutical, which is located in the northeastern part of the United States.

The sampling approach used for the present study was simple random sampling. According to Creswell (2002), the intent of simple random sampling is to choose a sample that will be representative of the target population. The target population for the present study was 400 district managers within Octagon Pharmaceutical. A random numbers table was used to select a random sample of district managers from the target population. The present study will attempt to generalize the findings to the target population after using simple random sampling.

The data for the present study was collected by means of an electronic questionnaire completed by district managers in the participating organization. Electronic questionnaires provide a more efficient form of data collection as compared to mailed questionnaires (Creswell, 2002). The questionnaire used (see Appendix A) was consistent with a previous questionnaire developed and used in multiple countries, including the United States, Canada, Australia, and the United Kingdom (Babakus et al., 1996; Cravens et al., 1993; Grant & Cravens, 1996; Piercy et al., 1999; Piercy et al., 2004) and different industries. The reliability and validity of the instrument and scales have been established in previous studies (Babakus et al., 1996; Cravens et al., 1993; Grant & Cravens, 1996; Piercy et al., 1999; Piercy et al., 2004), thus eliminating the need to pre-test the questionnaire for the purposes of this research. Analysis of reliability and validity of the instrument and scales for the present study was conducted using LISREL 8.80 (Jöreskog & Sörbom, 2006).

The analysis involved a correlation analysis of the constructs, followed by a multiple regression model and a structural equation model analysis. AMOS 6.0 (Arbuckle, 2005) software was used to conduct the analysis. According to Creswell (2002), multiple regressions are a statistical procedure for examining the combined relationship of multiple independent variables with a single dependent variable. In regression, the variation in the dependent variable is explained by the variance of each independent variable as well as the combined effect of all independent variables, designated by R^2 (Kline, 1998). In addition, a structural equation model analysis was completed to show how the predictor variables were operating and in order to explain the association in the outcome variable. Chapter 4 will present the data analysis and conclusions from the questionnaire results.

CHAPTER 4: RESULTS

The intent of this quantitative study, which uses an explanatory correlation research design, was to examine the relationships between sales management control, sales territory design, sales force performance, and sales organization effectiveness in sales organizations within the pharmaceutical industry. An electronic questionnaire was administered to collect data to measure the variables. Data was collected from district managers within sales organizations in the pharmaceutical industry. An overview of the data analysis and study results is presented in this chapter.

Data Analysis Process

The data analysis constituted four stages. The four stages of data analysis included pre-analysis data examination and data preparation, which was stage 1; validation of the measures, which was stage 2; a correlation analysis of the constructs and hypotheses, which was stage 3; and an assessment of the structural model and the path estimates, which was stage 4. The first section of this chapter presents the results of the first two stages of data analysis; subsequent sections present the results of the remaining two stages of the data analysis and results. The various analyses in the present study were undertaken using the SPSS 12.0, LISREL 8.80, and AMOS 6.0 computer programs. The measurement characteristics of the constructs included in the research model are initially examined; in the sections that follow the results of these initial analyses are described.

Stage 1: Pre-Analysis Data Examination and Data Preparation

Population and Sample Selection

This study was conducted at Octagon Pharmaceutical, which is located in the northeastern part of the United States. The random sample for this quantitative study, which used an explanatory correlation research design, was drawn from four separate operating companies within Octagon Pharmaceutical. The four operating companies employed 400 district managers at the time of this study. The random sample consisted of 200 district managers. Each of the 200 district managers were randomly selected for the sample using a random numbers table. Each district manager assigned to the random sample received an electronic questionnaire to complete. In total, 153 district managers returned the electronic questionnaire, resulting in a 77% response rate. The response rate exceeded the goal of 100 responses. The higher response rate is attributed to senior sales management of Octagon Pharmaceutical creating awareness and asking each manager to voluntarily complete the questionnaire. A missing value analysis resulted in two cases being deleted from the sample, making the final sample 151. Examination of the final sample revealed that more than two thirds of the participants (68%) had worked in the pharmaceutical industry for more than five years. The participants' profile is shown in Table 4.

Descriptive Statistics for the Individual Items

A total of 78 items were used to estimate the five constructs included in the suggested model. The constructs included four measures for sales management control (CONTROL), one each for satisfaction with sales territory design (Design) and sales force performance (OUTPERF), six for sales force behavioral performance (BEHPERF), and three for sales organization effectiveness (EFFECT). Consistent with previous sales management control research (Babakus et al., 1996; Piercy et al., 1999; Piercy et al., 2004) the construct measures in the present study were treated as continuous scales. Sales management control was measured using a 10-point scale that ranged from 1, meaning not at all, to 10, meaning to a great extent. Sales territory design was measured using a 7-point scale that ranged from 1, meaning not at all satisfied, to 7, meaning very satisfied.

Table 4.

Participants' Profile

Demographics	N	%
Operating company		
Not answered	1	0.66
Operating company A	29	19.21
Operating company B	44	29.14
Operating company C	1	0.66
Operating company D	76	50.33
Total responses	151	100
Tenure as a district manager		
Not answered	3	1.99
0-2 years	35	23.18
2-5 years	46	30.46
5-10 years	51	33.77
10-15 years	6	3.97
15+ years	10	6.62
Total responses	151	100

The sales force performance construct was measured using a 7-point scale that ranged from 1, meaning needs improvement, to 7, meaning outstanding. The sales organization effectiveness construct was measured using a 5-point scale that ranged from 1, meaning much worse, to 5, meaning much better. The descriptive statistics obtained are shown in Table 5.

Table 5.

Descriptive Statistics for Individual Items

Constructs and variables	Mean	*SD*
Construct 1: Behavior-based sales management control (CONTROL)		
Monitor		
1) Spend time with salespeople in the field.	8.85	1.290
2) Make joint calls with salespeople.	8.38	1.807
3) Regularly review call reports from salespeople.	7.58	1.998
4) Monitor the day-to-day activities of salespeople.	6.48	2.256
5) Observe the performance of salespeople in the field.	8.99	1.222
6) Pay attention to the extent to which salespeople travel.	6.40	2.245
7) Closely watch salespeople's expense accounts.	7.60	1.908
8) Pay attention to the credit terms that salespeople quote customers.	3.34	3.173
Scale mean	57.60	10.142

Table 5. (continued)

Direct	Mean	*SD*
1) Encourage salespeople to increase their sales results by rewarding them for their achievements.	8.50	1.591
2) Actively participate in training of salespeople on the job.	8.87	1.394
3) Regularly spend time coaching salespeople.	8.89	1.936
4) Discuss performance evaluations with salespeople.	8.70	1.657
5) Help salespeople develop their potential.	8.81	1.522
Scale mean	43.76	6.293

Evaluate		
1) Evaluate the number of sales calls made by salespeople.	7.36	1.860
2) Evaluate the profit contribution achieved by each salesperson.	5.87	2.782
3) Evaluate the sales results of each salesperson.	8.91	1.540
4) Evaluate the quality of sales presentations made by salespeople.	9.11	1.292
5) Evaluate the professional development of salespeople.	8.47	1.553
Scale mean	39.73	6.439

Table 5. (continued)

Reward	Mean	SD
1) Provide performance feedback to salespeople on a regular basis.	8.79	1.251
2) Compensate salespeople based on the quality of their sales activities.	7.40	2.098
3) Use the incentive compensation as the major means for motivating salespeople.	8.01	1.683
4) Make incentive compensation judgments based on the sales results achieved by salespeople.	7.28	2.466
5) Reward salespeople based on their sales results.	8.27	1.514
6) Use non-financial incentives to reward salespeople for their achievements.	7.82	2.000
7) Compensate salespeople based on the quantity of their sales activities.	5.85	2.773
Scale mean	53.42	9.046

Table 5. (continued)

Constructs and variables	Mean	SD
Construct 2: Satisfaction with sales territory design (TERR)		
1) The number of accounts in my territories.	5.23	1.257
2) The number of large accounts in my territories.	5.08	1.458
3) The sales productivity in my territories	4.75	1.270
4) The geographical size of my territories.	5.09	1.596
5) The number of calls made in my territories.	4.89	1.287
6) The amount of travel required in my territories.	5.03	1.641
7) The market potential in my territories.	5.12	1.291
8) The number of territories in my sales unit.	5.38	1.569
9) The assignment of salespeople to my territories.	5.21	1.359
10) The equivalence in workload across territories.	4.96	1.346
11) The overall design of my territories.	4.75	1.502
Scale mean	55.49	10.236
Construct 3: Sales Force Performance (OUTPERF)		
Outcome performance		
1) Producing a high market share for your company.	4.24	1.517
2) Making sales of those products with the highest profit margins.	4.17	1.577
3) Generating a high level of dollar sales.	4.32	1.463
4) Quickly generating sales of new company products/services.	3.87	1.650
5) Identifying and selling to major accounts.	4.73	1.270
6) Producing sales or blanket contracts with long-term profitability.	3.24	1.769
7) Exceeding all sales targets and objectives during the year.	3.94	1.462
Scale mean	28.51	7.624

Table 5. (continued)

Constructs and variables	Mean	SD
Construct 4: Sales force behavioral performance (BEHPERF)		
Technical knowledge		
1) Knowing the design and specifications of company products/services.	4.93	1.087
2) Knowing the application and functions of company products/services.	4.91	1.104
3) Keeping abreast of your company's production and technological developments.	4.17	1.335
Scale Mean	14.01	3.007
Adaptive selling		
1) Experimenting with different sales approaches.	4.45	1.360
2) Being flexible in the selling approaches used.	4.77	1.276
3) Adapting selling approaches from one customer to another.	4.70	1.221
4) Varying sales styles from situation to situation.	4.58	1.278
Scale Mean	46.53	9.217
Teamwork		
1) Generating considerable sales volume from team sales (sales jointly by two or more salespeople).	4.62	1.465
2) Building strong working relationships with other people in our company.	4.62	1.370
3) Working very closely with non-sales employees to close sales.	3.71	1.454
4) Coordinating very closely with other companies employees to handle post-sales problems and service.	3.68	1.647
5) Discussing selling strategies with people from various departments.	3.68	1.436
Scale Mean	20.29	5.826

Table 5. (continued)

Constructs and variables	Mean	SD
Sales Presentation		
1) Listening attentively to identify and understand the real concerns of customers.	4.44	1.325
2) Convincing customers that they understand their unique problems and concerns.	4.50	1.243
3) Using established contacts to develop new customers.	4.19	1.503
4) Communicating their sales presentation clearly and concisely.	4.98	0.948
5) Working out solutions to a customer's questions and objections.	4.72	1.073
Scale mean	22.83	4.773
Sales planning		
1) Planning each sales call.	4.43	1.334
2) Planning sales strategies for each customer.	4.44	1.247
3) Planning coverage of assigned territory/customer responsibility.	4.85	1.168
4) Planning daily activities.	4.75	1.179
Scale mean	18.48	4.271
Sales support		
1) Providing after sales service.	4.66	1.275
2) Checking on product delivery.	3.94	1.830
3) Handling customer complaints.	4.87	1.293
4) Follow up on product use.	4.91	1.256
5) Troubleshooting application problems.	4.03	1.667
6) Analyzing product use experience to identify new product/service ideas.	4.20	1.510
Scale mean	26.46	7.165

Table 5. (continued)

Constructs and variables	Mean	SD
Construct 5: Sales organization effectiveness (EFFECT)		
Sales and market share effectiveness		
1) Sales volume compared to your major competitor (past 24 months).	3.33	0.870
2) Market share compared to your major competitor.	3.30	0.916
3) Sales volume compared to sales unit objectives.	3.15	0.978
4) Market share compared to sales unit objectives.	3.18	0.895
Scale mean	12.97	2.915
Profitability		
1) Profitability compared to your major competitor.	3.26	0.991
2) Profitability compared to sales unit objectives.	3.17	0.912
Scale mean	6.43	1.809
Customer Satisfaction		
1) Customer satisfaction compared to your major competitors.	3.71	0.884
2) Customer satisfaction compared to sales unit objectives.	3.50	0.944
Scale mean	7.21	1.738

Missing Values

According to Tabachnick and Fidell (2001), "Missing data is one of the most pervasive problems in data analysis" (p. 58). Missing data can have serious effects on the reliability, validity, and generalizability of the data. Missing data can be indicative of lack of knowledge, fatigue, or sensitivity or it can be the result of a participant's interpretation that a question is irrelevant. According to Tabachnick and Fidell, when the number of missing cases is small (< 5%), it is common to exclude the cases from the analysis. In the present analysis, there were two cases with 100% and 40% missing values.

Before conducting an exploratory factor analysis, it must be determined if missing data is systematic (represents bias) or can be ignored. Missing data also has other important ramifications, especially in factor analysis. Factor analysis using listwise deletion should not be conducted unless the missing data is missing completely at random (MCAR).

Missing Value Analysis

The SPSS missing value analysis (MVA) was used to analyze the data for both missing at random (MAR) and MCAR data loss using an expectation maximization technique. Little's MCAR test (Little & Rubin, 2002), which is a chi-square test for missing completely at random, was used for the analysis. The results from Little's MCAR test suggested that the missing data is not MCAR and that the data loss pattern is systematic, χ^2 (92, $N = 153$) = 211.11, p = .000. Cases 107 and 121 were deleted and the analysis was rerun. After rerunning the analysis, Little's MCAR test result implied that the data is missing completely at random and is not systemic, χ^2 (83, $N = 151$) = 71.5, p = .812.

The SPSS MVA module also incorporates an expectation-maximization (EM) algorithm for the generation of imputed values used to fill in all the missing data. This technique was used to fill in the missing data in the dataset and is used later in the comparative fit index (CFI) analysis phase for comparison purposes. Because the data is

MCAR, listwise deletion is a better alternative than pairwise deletion because the latter may cause covariance matrix issues due to an unequal number of cases (Kline, 2005).

The AMOS application is unique in that it can be used to analyze data that includes missing data (Peters & Enders, 2002). AMOS incorporates a special form of maximum likelihood estimation (Special ML) which partitions all cases with the same missing data patterns. Peters and Enders found that this method for analyzing datasets with incomplete data "outperformed traditional (available case) methods" (as cited in Kline, 2005, p. 56). Tabachnick and Fidell (2001) suggested using both methods (with and without missing data) but favored the EM imputation method and listwise methods if the data can be ignored over mean substitution or pairwise deletion. Tabachnick and Fidell stated, "The decision about how to handle missing data is important. At best, the decision is among several bad alternatives" (p. 59).

Caution should be exercised with any method using a dataset with a high percentage of missing values (> 5%). Nunnally and Bernstein (1994) suggested that when a high percentage of missing values is evident, any of these methods may be unsatisfactory. Incorporating listwise deletion may be the best option for MCAR data because EM imputation may cause distorted coefficients of association and correlations (Kalton & Kasprzyk, 1982). In the present data set, the variable profit has 2.6% missing values and is left in the data set. The final sample size was 151.

Univariate Outliers

Outliers can cause serious problems for any regression based test such as structure equation modeling (SEM) (Tabachnick & Fidell, 2001). Due to distance separation from the normal data set, outliers tend to make the regression line deviate in the direction of

114

the outlier. Outliers can appear in both univariate and multivariate situations but Tabachnick and Fidell suggested first assessing univariate outliers. Outliers can be assessed using bivariate scatter plots or box plots. Examination of the box plots (see Appendix E) revealed that some variables have outliers that are between 1.5 and 3 box lengths from the top or bottom edge of the box. The data were reexamined to check for accuracy. All values were within the expected range, appeared to be a legitimate part of the sample, and were retained for the analysis.

The skewness and kurtosis of the variables were also examined. The variable called direct had a moderate negative skewness of -2.828 and kurtosis of 15.374. A normally distributed variable will have zero values for skewness and kurtosis. When a data distribution has negative skewness, the long tail is to the left, and the best strategy to transform a variable with moderate negative skewness is to conduct a square root transformation (Tabachnick & Fidell, 2001). The results of the square root transformation are shown in Table 6. The skewness and kurtosis of the new variable, direct2, are .624 and 1.474 respectively. The variable direct2 was used in the analysis. In summary, the data set used in the analysis contained 151 complete cases and one transformed variable, namely, direct2, in place of the skewed variable, namely, direct.

Table 6.

Variable Transformation

	N	Mean	Standard deviation	Skewness statistic	Std error	Kurtosis statistic	Std error
Direct	151	43.76	6.293	-2.828	0.197	15.374	0.392
Direct2	151	2.47	1.067	0.624	0.197	1.474	0.392
Valid N (listwise)	151						

Stage 2: Validation of the Measures

The model of sales organization effectiveness is dependent on sales management control, sales territory design, sales force behavioral performance, and sales force outcome performance. Babakus et al. (1996) and Piercy et al. (1999) employed the same model using different samples. That sales outcome performance will have a positive effect on sales organization effectiveness was anticipated. Similarly, sales force outcome performance is dependent on sales force behavioral performance, sales management control, sales territory design, and a residual disturbance term. The residual error term, also called disturbance term, reflects unexplained variance or the effect of unmeasured variables plus measurement error (Tabachnick & Fidell, 2001).

Sales force behavioral performance is dependent on sales management control, sales territory design, and a disturbance term. Sales territory design is dependent on sales management control and a residual disturbance term that represents all the variation in sales territory design not explained by the latent, exogenous variable, sales management control. The disturbance term is assumed to be independent of the exogenous variable

116

and is also assumed to be independent of the disturbance terms attached to sales force behavioral performance, sales force outcome performance, and sales organization effectiveness. The basic model of sales organization effectiveness is shown diagrammatically in Figure 3. The theoretical, latent variables of interest are shown in ellipsis.

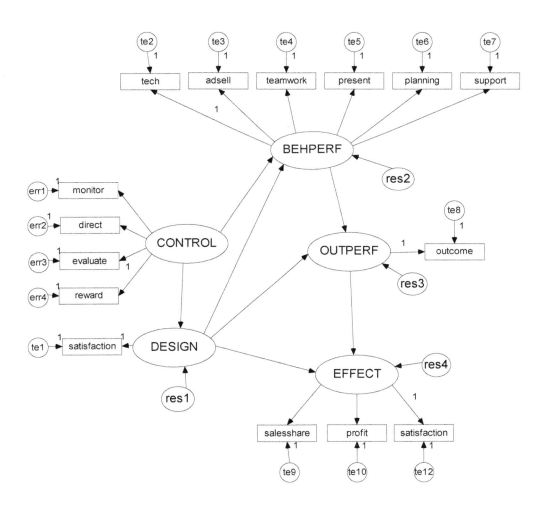

Figure 3. Basic model of sales organization effectiveness (*N* = 151).

The model has five latent constructs. Multiple indicators measure three of these constructs, which is a recommended practice in structural equation modeling (Kline, 2005). First, indicators are not generally free from the effects of random error, so their scores are not perfectly reliable. Second, scores may not be perfectly valid, so not all of the systematic part of an observed variable's variance reflects the construct.

Two constructs, or latent variables, have only one indicator each. When a construct is measured by one observed variable, Jöreskog and Sörbom (1989) suggested that it is reasonable that the reliability of that measure is not equal to 1.00 or a perfect measure. Error variances may be computed as the variance times .15 to approximate 85% reliability. These are also known as start values. In the present model, the error variances for design and outcome performance were computed as 15.716 (104.78 × .15) and 8.719 (58.13 × .15) respectively.

Assessing Reliability and Validity of Constructs and Indicators

One of the most important advantages offered by latent variable analyses is the opportunity to assess the reliability and validity of variables (Kline, 2005). In general, reliability refers to consistency of measurement, and validity refers to the extent to which an instrument measures what it is intended to measure (Creswell, 2002). For example, a survey is reliable if it provides essentially the same set of responses for a group of participants upon repeated administration. Similarly, if a scale is developed to measure sales organization effectiveness and scores on the scale do, in fact, reflect participants' underlying levels of sales behavior performance, the scale is valid (Kline, 2005). For both reliability and validity, a number of different ways that reliability and validity may be measured exist. Estimates for the present study were obtained using the LISREL 8.80 (Jöreskog & Sörbom, 2006).

The reliability of an *indicator*, or observed variable, is defined as the square of the correlation (squared multiple correlation or SMC) between a latent factor and that indicator. For instance, if one looks at Table 7, the standardized loading for the path between monitor and control is .722 and the reliability is .522. Looking at the range of indicator reliabilities, many have relatively high reliability (.60 and above), and several have low reliability, like planning with an indicator reliability of .180.

Table 7.

Composite Reliability and Variance Extracted Estimates

Construct and indicators	Standardized loading	Indicator reliability	Error variance	t-value	Composite reliability	Variance extracted
Control					0.835	0.563
Monitor	0.722	0.522	0.278	8.817		
Direct2	0.494	0.244	0.506	5.699		
Evaluate	0.714	0.510	0.286	8.707		
Reward	0.700	0.490	0.300	8.515		
Behavior					0.865	0.460
Performance						
Tech	0.902	0.814	0.098	13.975		
Adaptive	0.998	0.996	0.002	16.592		
Teamwork	0.481	0.232	0.519	6.244		

Table 7. (continued)

Construct and indicators	Standardized loading	Indicator reliability	Error variance	t-value	Composite reliability	Variance extracted
Presentation	0.556	0.309	0.444	7.361		
Planning	0.424	0.180	0.576	5.430		
Support	0.366	0.134	0.634	4.638		
Effect					0.825	0.613
Effective	0.778	0.606	0.222	8.733		
Profit	0.640	0.410	0.360	7.347		
Satisfaction	0.663	0.439	0.337	7.582		

Correlations

	Control	BehPerf	Effect
Control	1		
Behavior Performance	0.225	1	
Effect	0.199	0.182	1

Squared

Correlations

	Control	BehPerf	Effect
Control	1		
Behavior Performance	0.051	1	
Effect	0.040	0.033	1

Composite reliability has been computed for each latent factor included in the model. This index is similar to the coefficient and reflects the internal consistency of the indicators measuring a particular factor (Fornell & Larcker, 1981). Both the composite reliability and the variance extracted estimates are shown in Table 7. Fornell and Larcker (1981) recommend a minimum composite reliability of .60. An examination of the composite reliabilities revealed that all variables meet that minimum acceptable level.

The variance extracted estimates assess the amount of variance explained by an underlying factor in relation to the amount of variance due to measurement error. For instance, the variance extracted estimate for control was .563, meaning that 56.3% of the variance is explained by the skill construct, and 43.7% is due to measurement error. Fornell and Larcker (1981) suggested that constructs should exhibit estimates of .50 or larger. Estimates of less than .50 indicate that the variance due to measurement error is larger than the variance captured by the factor. The variance extracted estimates for control and effect meet this minimum threshold, so the validity of these latent constructs as well as the associated constructs is acceptable. It should also be noted that Hatcher (1994) cautions that the variance extracted estimate test is conservative; reliabilities can be acceptable even if variance extracted estimates are less than .50, as is the case with behavior performance with a variance extracted estimate .460.

Convergent validity is present when different instruments are used to measure the same construct and scores from these different instruments are strongly correlated (Anderson & Gerbing, 1988). In contrast, *discriminant validity* is present when different instruments are used to measure different constructs and the measures of these different constructs are weakly correlated.

121

In the present study, convergent validity was assessed by reviewing the t-tests for the factor loadings. If all the factor loadings for the indicators were greater than twice their standard errors, the parameter estimates demonstrated convergent validity. That all t-tests are significant suggested that all indicators were effectively measuring the same construct (Anderson & Gerbing, 1988). Consider the convergent validity of the six indicators that measure behavior performance, technical (tech), adaptive, teamwork, presentation, planning and support. The results (see Table 7) show that the t-values for these six indicators range from 4.638 to 16.592, critical value $t = 3.29$ for $p = .001$. These results supported the convergent validity of technical (tech), adaptive, teamwork, presentation, planning and support as measures of behavioral performance.

Discriminant validity was assessed using the variance extracted test. Constructs were evaluated by comparing the variance extracted estimates for two factors, and compared with the square of the correlation between the two factors. Discriminant validity is demonstrated if both variance extracted estimates are greater than the squared correlation. In the present study, the correlation between the factors control and behavioral performance was .225; the squared correlation was .051. The variance extracted estimate was .563 for control and .460 for behavioral performance. Because the variance extracted estimates are greater than the square of the interfactor correlation, the test supports the discriminant validity of these two factors. Examination of the other variance extracted estimates and squared correlation coefficients supported the discriminant validity of the model.

In the first two stages, the results of an assessment of the constructs and the measurement model were discussed. All constructs in the research model were found to

122

have good measurement properties. The sequence of analysis included a correlation analysis of the constructs and hypotheses in stage 3, followed by the development and interpretation of a structural equation model in stage 4. The next sections will discuss stages 3 and 4 of the data analysis and results.

Stage 3: Correlation Analysis of Constructs and Hypotheses

The constructs evaluated in the present study were the following: sales organization effectiveness; sales management control; sales force performance in terms of both behavior and outcome; and sales territory design. The proposed relationships among these constructs are presented by the following null hypotheses:

$H1_0$: No significant correlation exists between the level of sales force behavioral performance and the level of sales force outcome performance.

$H2_0$: No significant correlation exists between the level of sales force outcome performance and the level of sales organization effectiveness.

$H3_0$: No significant correlation exists between the extent of behavior-based sales management control and the level of sales force behavioral performance.

$H4_0$: No significant correlation exists between the extent of behavior-based sales management control and the level of satisfaction with sales territory design.

$H5_0$: No significant correlation exists between the extent of satisfaction with sales territory design and the level of sales organization effectiveness.

$H6_0$: No significant correlation exists between the extent of satisfaction with sales territory design and the level of sales force behavioral performance.

$H7_0$: No significant correlation exists between the extent of satisfaction with sales territory design and the level of sales force outcome performance.

Each null hypothesis was tested. A significance level of .05 was used for all statistical tests. In each case, the null hypothesis was rejected if the correlations probability is equal or below .05 level of significance. In the following sections, the results of each test are discussed. The correlation matrix shown in Table 8 provides an evaluation of the results of the hypotheses tests.

Null Hypothesis 1

$H1_0$ suggests that no significant correlation exists between the level of sales force behavioral performance and the level of sales force outcome performance. The results suggest that the null hypothesis be rejected at a .05 level of significance. This study found a significant positive correlation between outcome performance and the components of behavioral performance: technical knowledge ($r = .29, p < .05$), sales presentations ($r = .48, p < .05$), adaptive selling ($r = .37, p < .05$), teamwork ($r = .39, p < .05$), sales planning ($r = .37, p < .05$), and sales support ($r = .42, p < .05$). As a result, the alternative hypothesis ($H1_a$) is accepted: A significant correlation exists between the level of sales force behavioral performance and the level of sales force outcome performance.

Null Hypothesis 2

$H2_0$ suggests no significant correlation exists between the level of sales force outcome performance and the level of sales organization effectiveness. The results suggest that the null hypothesis be rejected at a .05 level of significance. This study found a significant positive correlation between sales force outcome performance and sales organization effectiveness, $r = .45, p < .05$. As a result, the alternative hypothesis ($H2_a$) is accepted: A significant correlation exists between the level of sales force outcome performance and the level of sales organization effectiveness.

Table 8.

Correlations, Means and Standard Deviations (N = 151)

	Monitor	Direct	Evaluate	Reward	Design	Tech	Adaptive	Teamwork	Present	Planning	Support	OutcomeP	Effective	Profit	Satisfaction
Monitor	1														
Direct	0.329*	1													
Evaluate	0.526*	0.368*	1												
Reward	0.514*	0.355*	0.480*	1											
Design	0.102	-0.05	0.151	0.097	1										
Tech	0.083	0.08	0.135	0.094	0.352*	1									
Adaptive	0.13	0.103	0.182*	0.186*	0.386*	0.902*	1								
Teamwork	0.223*	0.1	0.151	0.302*	0.210*	0.425*	0.526*	1							
Present	0.220*	0.018	0.194*	0.276*	0.358*	0.451*	0.633*	0.588*	1						
Planning	0.205*	0.07	0.209*	0.276*	0.325*	0.318*	0.482*	0.377*	0.612*	1					
Support	0.214*	0.067	0.174*	0.282*	0.249*	0.319*	0.409*	0.580*	0.529*	0.471*	1				
OutcomeP	0.174*	0.032	0.180*	0.358*	0.323*	0.286*	0.365*	0.391*	0.483*	0.365*	0.417*	1			
Effective	0.101	0.093	0.049	0.187*	0.265*	0.132*	0.187*	0.175*	0.259*	0.273*	0.249*	0.454*	1		
Profit	-0.051	0.053	0.03	0.048	0.088	-0.06	-0.016	0.09	0.09	0.074	0.09	0.182*	0.467*	1	
Satisfaction	0.179*	0.156	0.139	0.084	0.221*	0.303*	0.303*	0.235*	0.257*	0.102	0.266*	0.279*	0.437*	0.371*	1
Mean	57.6	43.76	39.73	53.42	55.49	14.01	46.53	20.29	22.83	18.48	26.46	28.51	12.97	6.43	7.21
SD	10.142	6.293	6.439	9.046	10.236	3.007	9.217	5.826	4.773	4.271	7.165	7.624	2.915	1.809	1.738

* Significant at $p \leq .05$

Null Hypothesis 3

$H3_0$ suggests no significant correlation exists between the extent of behavior-based sales management control and the level of sales force behavioral performance. The results suggest that the null hypothesis be rejected at a .05 level of significance. The results from this study found a significant positive correlation between behavior-based sales management control and salesperson behavioral performance, $r = .40$, $p < .05$. However, the correlations between sales management monitoring, directing, evaluating and rewarding activities and the six measures of behavioral performance indicate mixed results. Sales manager monitoring activities show strong relationships with teamwork ($r = .22$, $p < .05$), presentation ($r = .22$, $p < .05$), planning ($r = .21$, $p < .05$) and support ($r =$

.21, $p < .05$). Similarly, evaluating activities show strong relationships with adaptive selling ($r = .18$, $p < .05$), sales presentation ($r = .19$, $p < .05$), planning ($r = .21$, $p < .05$), and support ($r = .17$, $p < .05$). Rewarding activities show strong relationships with adaptive selling ($r = .19$, $p < .05$), teamwork ($r = .30$, $p < .05$), sales presentation ($r = .28$, $p < .05$), planning ($r = .28$, $p < .05$) and support ($r = .28$, p .05). In contrast, directing activities show no significant relationships with any of the measures of behavioral performance. Thus, there is mixed support for the hypothesis that a significant correlation exists between the extent of behavior-based sales management control and the level of sales force behavioral performance. While the overall correlation between sales management control and behavioral performance is significant and positive, not all the elements of behavior-based sales management control and each of the dimensions of sales force behavioral performance exhibit significant correlations.

Null Hypothesis 4

$H4_0$ suggests no significant correlation exists between the extent of behavior-based sales management control and the level of satisfaction with sales territory design. The results did not contradict the null hypothesis. The overall correlations between sales management control and sales territory design indicated the two variables were not correlated with the correlation coefficient, $r = .15$, $p > .05$. The correlations between the individual measures of sales management control; sales management monitoring ($r = .102$, $p > .05$), directing ($r = -.051$, $p > .05$), evaluating ($r = .151$, $p > .05$), and rewarding activities ($r = .097$, $p > .05$) indicate no significant relationships with sales territory design. Therefore, the findings in the present study failed to reject the null hypothesis.

Null Hypothesis 5

$H5_0$ suggests no significant correlation exists between the extent of satisfaction with sales territory design and the level of sales organization effectiveness. The results did not contradict the null hypothesis. The study found a positive but not significant correlation between sales territory design and sales organization effectiveness, $r = .30, p > .05$. The individual measures of sales and market share effectiveness (effective) ($r = .265, p < .05$) and customer satisfaction (satisfaction) ($r = .221, p < .05$) showed significant positive correlations with sales territory design. The individual measure of sales organization effectiveness with respect to profit ($r = .088, p > .05$) does not show a significant relationship with sales territory design. Therefore, the findings in the present study failed to reject the null hypothesis.

Null Hypothesis 6

$H6_0$ suggests no significant correlation exists between the extent of satisfaction with sales territory design and the level of sales force behavioral performance. The results suggest that the null hypothesis be rejected at a .05 level of significance. A significant positive correlation between satisfaction with sales territory design and sales force behavioral performance is apparent, $r = .45, p < .05$. Therefore, the alternative hypothesis ($H6_a$) is accepted: A significant correlation exists between the extent of satisfaction with the sales territory design and the level of sales force behavioral performance.

Null Hypothesis 7

$H7_0$ suggests no significant correlation exists between the extent of satisfaction with sales territory design and the level of sales force outcome performance. The results suggest that the null hypothesis be rejected at a .05 level of significance. A significant

127

positive correlation between satisfaction with sales territory design and sales force outcome performance is apparent, $r = .32, p < .05$. Therefore, the alternative hypothesis ($H7_a$) is accepted: A significant correlation exists between the extent of satisfaction with sales territory design and the level of sales force outcome performance.

Stage 4: Assessing the Structural Model and Path Estimates

Correlation measures the strength of a linear relationship between an explanatory variable and a response, but it cannot measure the relationship between a response and more than one explanatory variable or explain and predict causal relationships (Creswell, 2002). Regression is better than correlation for explaining and predicting causal relationships; however, regression is limited in its ability to predict relationships between unobserved, latent constructs, such as behavior-based sales management control and sales force behavioral performance. Goldberger (1973) considered three situations in which structural equation models are more useful than regression models: (a) when the observed variables contain measurement errors and the interesting relationship is among the latent variables, (b) when there is interdependence of simultaneous causation among the observed variables, and (c) when important explanatory variables have not been observed, or are omitted variables. To control for differential measurement errors in the estimation of latent variable parameters, a structural equation model (SEM) was developed and tested.

Structural Equation Model Analysis

Estimates of parameters were obtained by using AMOS 6.0 (Arbuckle, 2005). The first step in the analysis was to establish a baseline model. The results of this model indicate that the results are admissible, $\chi^2 (86, N = 151) = 258.81, p = .0001$; root mean square error of approximation (RMSEA) = .116, 95% confidence interval (CI.95) = .100, .132. Goodness-of-fit index (GFI) and comparative fit index (CFI) is .770 and .809 respectively. Chi-square is a measure of the compatibility of the data with the hypothesis. A chi-square value this large relative to the degrees of freedom indicates a poor fit between the estimated and actual covariance matrices (Arbuckle, 2005). The comparative fit index (CFI) compares the covariance matrix predicted by the model to the observed covariance matrix and compares the null model with the observed covariance matrix to measure the percent of lack of fit that can be accounted for by going from the null model to the proposed SEM model. CFI and RMSEA are among the measures least affected by sample size (Fan, Thompson, & Wang, 1999). CFI varies from 0 to 1. A CFI close to 1 indicates a very good fit.

The RMSEA is a measure of the closeness of fit, with values less than .05 indicating good model fit, and values up to .08 indicating reasonable model fit (Browne & Cudeck, 1993; Hun & Bentler, 1999). Steiger (1990), Browne and Cudeck (1993), and MacCallum, Browne, and Sugawara (1996) suggested that a confidence interval (CI) be calculated that includes values between 0 and .05 to indicate the possibility of good fit. The goodness-of-fit index (GFI) was developed by Jöreskog and Sörbom (1984) and deals with error in reproducing the variance-covariance matrix. Values for the GFI range from 0 to 1 with 1 being a perfect fit. Values greater than .90 are considered excellent (Bentler & Chou, 1987).

The structural portion of the model was completely identified, so the lack of fit was in the measurement portion of the model (Arbuckle, 2005). The modification indices in AMOS provided a powerful tool for detecting the model's parameters, which according to Arbuckle, if set free, improve the fit of a model. An examination of the modification indices (see Appendix F) indicate that the covariance between several disturbance terms be set free. According to Arbuckle, this should result in an improvement in the fit of the model. However, any change in a path should have substantive merit for the model. In other words, any changes in the model should be supported by the underlying theory. For instance, if the model were to be re-estimated with the path between theta epsilon 7 (te7) and theta epsilon 8 (te8) set free, the overall chi-square statistic should drop by at least 8.962, and the value of the estimate itself to approximately 10.178. Covariance between the reporting errors for measures of sales force behavioral performance were set free and the model was re-estimated.

The re-estimated model (see Appendix G) resulted in a chi-square statistic closer to the degrees of freedom, $\chi^2 (76, N = 120) = 86.19, p = .199$. A chi-square statistic close to the degrees of freedom indicates a good fit between the estimated and actual covariance matrices (Arbuckle, 2005). Other goodness-of-fit measures support the acceptance of this model, RMSEA = .030, $CI_{.95} = .0001, .057$. The CFI and GFI for the re-estimated model is .989 and .934 respectively. Therefore, the model (see Appendix H) is an excellent fit to the data.

Measurement model parameter estimates are standardized regression coefficients (Arbuckle, 2005). A standardized regression coefficient or beta coefficient is the estimate of an analysis performed on variables that have been standardized so that they have a variance of 1 (Arbuckle, 2005). According to Arbuckle (2005), standardized regression coefficients indicate which independent variables is the best predictor of the dependent variable in multiple regression analysis. Standardized regression coefficients are labeled β. The measurement model parameter estimates are shown in Table 9. In order of magnitude, monitor (β = .724, p = .0001) is the best predictor of control followed by reward (β = .717, p = .0001), evaluate (β = .703, p = .0001) and direct (β = .478, p = .0001). For the construct sales force behavioral performance in order of magnitude, present (β = .837, p = .0001) is the best predictor followed by adsell/adaptive (β = .746, p = .0001), planning (β = .708, p = .0001), teamwork (β = .695, p = .0001), and support (β = .655, p = .0001). For the construct, sales organization effectiveness, sales share (β = .849, p = .0001) is the best predictor followed by satisfaction (β = .546, p = .0001).

The unstandardized regression coefficients and coefficients of determination are shown in Table 10. With respect to sales organization effectiveness, 32.1% is explained by sales management control, sales territory design, sales force behavioral performance, and sales force outcome performance. Behavior-based sales management control has a significant positive effect on sales force behavioral performance, as does sales territory design. Similarly, sales force behavioral performance has a significant positive effect on sales force outcome performance; in turn, sales force outcome performance has a significant positive influence on sales organization effectiveness. Confirmation for the current model is mixed due to the presence of non-significant paths in the model. Behavior-based sales management control has a positive but not significant influence on sales territory design; sales territory design has positive but not significant relationship to sales force outcome performance and sales organization effectiveness.

Table 9.

Measurement Model Parameter Estimates (N = 151)

Variables		Standardized		Standard	Critical	*p*-	
Latent	Observed	Estimate	Estimate	Error	Ratio	value	Reliability
Control							
	monitor	0.724	1.132	0.164	6.897	0.000**	0.524
	direct	0.478	0.463	0.093	4.972	0.000**	0.228
	evaluate	0.703	0.699	0.103	6.808	0.000**	0.495
	reward	0.717	1.000				0.514
Design							
	satisfaction	0.921	1.000				0.846
Behavioral							
performance							
	tech	0.603	1.000				0.363
	adsell						
	(adaptive)	0.746	3.788	0.285	13.274	0.000**	0.557
	teamwork	0.695	2.231	0.360	6.203	0.000**	0.483
	present	0.837	2.202	0.348	6.325	0.000**	0.701
	planning	0.708	1.666	0.305	5.459	0.000**	0.501
	support	0.655	2.585	0.453	5.711	0.000**	0.429

Table 9. (continued)

Variables Latent	Observed	Standardized Estimate	Estimate	Standard Error	Critical Ratio	p-value	Reliability
Outcome performance							
	outcome	0.921	1.000				0.849
Effect							
	sales share	0.849	2.608	0.503	5.188	0.000**	0.720
	profit	0.541	1.033	0.213	4.850	0.000**	0.293
	satisfaction	0.546	1.000				0.297

**Significant at $p < .001$

Table 10.

Structural Coefficients in Metric Form (N = 151)

	Design	BehPerf	OutPerf	Effect
Control	0.223	0.091*		
Sales territory design (Design)		0.081*	0.093	0.014
Behavioral performance (BehPerf)			2.103*	
Outcome performance (OutPerf)				0.067*
Sales organization effectiveness (Effect)				
Coefficient of determination	0.024	0.325	0.374	0.321

* Significant at $p \leq .05$

The standardized coefficients are shown in Table 11. The standardized coefficient results indicate sales force outcome performance is a better predictor of sales organization effectiveness than sales territory design. Sales force behavioral performance is the best predictor of sales force outcome performance followed by sales territory design. The best predictor of sales force behavioral performance is sales territory design followed by control. The results indicate that for this sample, sales territory design does not have a large direct influence on sales organization effectiveness.

Table 11.

Structural Coefficients in Standard Form (N = 151)

	Design	BehPerf	OutPerf	Effect
Control	0.154	0.326*		
Sales Territory Design (Design)		0.420*	0.124	0.143
Behavioral Performance (BehPerf)			0.543*	
Outcome Performance (OutPerf)				0.497*

* Significant at $p \leq .05$

The direct and indirect effects of sales territory design, sales management control, sales force outcome performance, and sales force behavioral performance on sales organization effectiveness are shown in Table 12. These data suggest that sales organization effectiveness is influenced most by sales force outcome performance. Sales territory design influence on sales organization effectiveness has a direct relationship with sales force behavioral performance. The next largest influence on sales organization effectiveness is from sales force behavioral performance. The direct relationship between sales force behavioral performance and sales force outcome performance and the indirect relationship with sales organization effectiveness through sales force outcome

performance are both positive and significant.

Table 12.

Effects of Independents on Sales Organization Effectiveness

Independents	Direct Effect	Indirect Effect	Total Effect
Sales territory design (Design)	0.143	0.018	0.318
Sales management control system (Control)	-	0.020	0.137
Sales force outcome performance (OutPerf)	0.497	-	0.497
Sales force behavioral performance (BehPerf)	-	0.141	0.270

Summary

Chapter 4 provided a detailed overview of the study sample, data analysis, and results. A random sample of 200 district managers was included in the study. All district managers were employed in the pharmaceutical industry. Each of the district managers within the random sample received an electronic questionnaire to complete. In total, 153 district managers completed the questionnaire, resulting in a response rate of 77%, which was higher than expected.

The data analysis and model assessment included four stages. Stage 1 included a pre-analysis data examination and data preparation stage and resulted in 151 complete cases, and one transformed variable, direct2. Stage 2 validated the construct measures and demonstrated reliability and validity of the study variables. Stage 3 included a correlation analysis of the constructs and hypotheses. Stage 4 assessed the structural equation model and the path estimates and confirmed that the model is an excellent fit to the data.

The results of the correlation analysis found that a significant relationship exists between sales force behavioral performance and sales force outcome performance. Sales force outcome performance has a significant influence on sales organization effectiveness. Behavioral-based sales management control is strongly related to sales force behavioral performance. Satisfaction with sales territory design has a significant relationship with sales force behavioral performance.

In contrast, while the overall correlation between sales management control and sales force behavioral performance is significant and positive, not all the elements of behavioral-based sales management control and each dimension of sales force behavioral performance exhibit significant correlations. In addition, correlations between sales management control individual measures, monitoring, directing, evaluating, and rewarding activities indicate no significant relationships with sales territory design. Last, the correlation between satisfaction with sales territory design and sales organization effectiveness is not significant.

The results of the structural equation model suggested that sales force behavioral performance has a significant relationship to sales force outcome performance. Sales force outcome performance has the greatest influence on sales organization effectiveness. Satisfaction with sales territory has a positive influence on sales organization effectiveness, mainly through its significant relationship with sales force behavioral performance. Finally, behavioral-based sales management control has a significant influence on sales force behavior performance. Chapter 5 provides a detailed summary of the conclusions, implications, and recommendations reached in this study.

CHAPTER 5: CONCLUSIONS AND RECOMMENDATIONS

Limited research exists about what factors influence sales force performance in pharmaceutical sales organizations. Sales leaders within pharmaceutical sales organizations therefore, lack information to improve sales force performance. Past research from other industries (Churchill et al., 1985; Mount & Barrick, 1995; Vinchur et al., 1998) attempted to help identify reliable and valid predictors of sales force performance by studying the determinants of individual salesperson's performance. However, the hypothesized predictors explained little of the variation in sales force performance.

The purpose of the present quantitative study, using an explanatory correlation research design, was to examine the relationships between sales management control, sales territory design, sales force performance, and sales organization effectiveness in sales organizations within the pharmaceutical industry. Examining these constructs within sales organizations in the pharmaceutical industry extended and built upon the findings of the research about sales force management control by distinguishing between behavior-based and outcome-based sales management control approaches in a new sample (Anderson & Oliver, 1987; Oliver & Anderson, 1994). In addition, the constructs evaluated in the present study were found in past studies examining sales management processes (e.g. Babakus et al., 1996; Cravens et al., 1993, Piercy et al., 1999), and modeling the interrelationships between them followed the general propositions formulated by Walker et al. (1979). According to Babakus et al. (1996), Walker et al. research is considered the foundation for much of the contemporary sales and sales management research.

The scope of the present study was limited to district managers employed by Octagon Pharmaceutical, which is located in the northeastern part of the United States. District managers were considered first-line sales managers within pharmaceutical sales organizations (Curry & Frost, 2001). The present study examined the influence of sales management control, sales territory design, and sales force performance on sales organization effectiveness in four separate operating companies within Octagon Pharmaceutical. The data collection activities associated with the present study was limited to district managers within the four operating companies of Octagon Pharmaceutical. The remainder of chapter 5 will discuss the conclusions, implications, and recommendations based on the research findings.

Conclusions

This study was designed to respond to the following research question: What relationships exist between sales management control, sales territory design, sales force performance, and sales organization effectiveness in the pharmaceutical industry? Seven hypotheses were tested to answer the research question. These hypotheses were tested in previous research (Babakus et al., 1996; Piercy et al., 1999) with different sample populations. In addition, to control for differential measurement errors in the estimation of latent variable parameters, a structural equation model (SEM) was developed and tested. The remainder of this section will discuss the conclusions from each stage of the data analysis, the pre-analysis data examination and data preparation, the validation of measures, the correlation analysis of constructs, and the assessment of the structural model and path estimates for the present study.

Pre-analysis Data Examination and Data Preparation

The participants in the present study were district managers employed by different operating companies within a pharmaceutical company located in the northeastern part of the United States. The pharmaceutical company consisted of four separate operating companies with different customer and product portfolios. Each operating company had different sales management personnel. The study participants varied by operating company, performance, industry tenure, and district manager experience.

The sample for the present study was chosen from a list of 400 district managers using simple random sampling. The random sample included 200 district managers. The random sample of 200 district managers was selected using a random numbers table. Each of the district managers within the random sample received an electronic questionnaire to complete. In total, 153 district managers completed the questionnaire, resulting in a response rate of 77%, which was higher than expected. A missing value analysis resulted in two cases being deleted from the sample, making the final sample 151. A disproportionate share of the sample, 68%, had worked more than five years in the pharmaceutical industry. Based on the sample characteristics, size, and sample methodology, simple random sampling, the present study was deemed representative of the target population studied.

Validation of the Measures

The model used for the present study had five latent constructs. Both composite reliability and construct validity were examined for each of the constructs. Composite reliability was computed for each latent factor and was found to meet the minimum acceptable level. Validity was examined using variance extracted estimates. Variance extracted estimates assess the amount of variance explained by an underlying factor in relation to the amount of variance due to measurement error. The variance extracted estimates for the present study met the minimal threshold, so the validity of all latent constructs were deemed acceptable.

In addition, convergent and discriminant validity was assessed for the model used in the present study. Convergent validity is present when different instruments are used to measure the same constructs and scores from these different instruments are strongly correlated. Discriminant validity is present when different instruments are used to measure different constructs and the measures of these different constructs are weakly correlated. That all t-tests were significant showed that all indicators were effectively measuring the same construct, thus demonstrating the convergent validity of the model. Examination of the variance extracted estimates and squared correlation coefficients supported the discriminant validity of the model.

In summary, all of the constructs in the research model have good measurement properties. The next section will present the conclusions from the correlation analysis in terms of the hypotheses and structural equation model.

Hypothesis One

$H1_a$ suggested that sales force behavioral performance is positively associated with sales force outcome performance. This hypothesis is strongly supported by high, positive correlations between sales force outcome performance and various components of behavioral performance, including technical knowledge, sales presentations, adaptive selling, teamwork, sales planning, and sales support. These results are consistent with past research examining the same constructs in different industries (Babakus et al., 1996;

Piercy, 1999). In addition, the direction of this hypothesis confirmed the findings of both Cravens et al. (1993) and Grant and Cravens (1996) who found a positive relationship between behavioral and outcome sales force performance in sales organizations outside the pharmaceutical industry employing behavioral-based sales force control approaches. This evidence is strongly suggestive of a high degree of association in the expected direction between behavioral and outcome performance.

Hypothesis Two

$H2_a$ proposed that sales force outcome performance is positively associated with sales organization effectiveness. The research also found substantial support in the significant positive correlation between sales force outcome performance and sales organization effectiveness. The direction of this hypothesis confirmed the findings of Cravens et al. (1993) and Grant and Cravens (1996) who found a positive relationship between outcome performance and financial effectiveness in sales organizations outside the pharmaceutical industry practicing behavioral-based sales management control. In addition, these results were consistent with past research examining the same constructs (Babakus et al., 1996; Piercy et al., 1999) in different samples.

Hypothesis Three

$H3_a$ suggested that the extent of behavior-based sales management control is positively related to the level of sales force behavioral performance. Overall, the correlation between sales management control and sales force behavioral performance was significant. However, the correlations between sales management monitoring, directing, evaluating, and rewarding activities and the six measures of sales force behavioral performance indicate mixed results. Sales manager monitoring activities show

142

strong relationships with teamwork, presentation, planning and support. Similarly, evaluating activities showed strong relationships with adaptive selling, sales presentation, planning, and support. Rewarding activities showed strong relationships with adaptive selling, teamwork, sales presentation, planning, and support. In contrast, directing activities show no significant relationships with any of the measures of sales force behavioral performance. Thus, mixed support for the hypothesis that the extent of behavior-based sales management control is related to the level of sales force behavioral performance.

While the overall correlation between sales management control and sales force behavioral performance is significant and positive, not all the elements of behavior-based sales management control and each of the dimensions of sales force behavioral performance exhibited significant correlations. However, while the hypothesis did not receive total support, convincing evidence existed for the expected positive relationship between most elements of behavior-based sales management control and most of the dimensions of sales force behavioral performance. These results were consistent with past research testing the same hypothesis in different samples (Babakus et al., 1996; Piercy et al., 1999).

Hypothesis Four

$H4_a$ proposed that behavior-based sales management control is positively associated to the degree of satisfaction with sales territory design. The overall correlation between behavior-based sales management control and sales territory design was positive. However, the correlations between sales management monitoring, directing, evaluating, and rewarding activities indicated no significant relationships with sales territory design. Thus, $H4_a$ was not supported. This result contradicted Babakus et al. (1996) and Piercy et al. (1999) findings from different industries. Babakus et al. research found a significant correlation between behavior-based sales management control and sales territory design. Piercy et al. findings resulted in the hypothesis receiving convincing support for the directing and evaluating components of behavior-based sales management control, but not for the monitoring and rewarding components.

Hypothesis Five

$H5_a$ suggested a link between satisfaction with sales territory design and sales organization effectiveness. The overall correlation between these measures is positive. The individual measures, sales and market share effectiveness and customer satisfaction were high and positive, but the correlation between sales territory design and profit did not show a significant relationship. Thus, the hypothesis did not receive total support. These results were not completely consistent with the results from Babakus et al. (1996) and Piercy et al. (1999) from different industries. Both Babakus et al. and Piercy et al.'s research found support for the relationship of satisfaction with sales territory design and individual measures of sales and market share effectiveness and customer satisfaction. However, unlike Babakus et al. and Piercy et al.'s research, this research did not support the relationship between satisfaction with sales territory design and the individual measure of profit.

Hypothesis Six

$H6_a$ proposed that the extent of satisfaction with sales territory design is positively correlated to the level of sales force behavioral performance. The overall correlation between these measures was high and positive. For the individual measures, the correlations between technical knowledge, sales presentation, adaptive selling, teamwork, sales planning and support showed strong relationships with sales territory design. This hypothesis was strongly supported. Satisfaction with sales territory design correlated significantly and positively with all the measures of sales force behavioral performance. The results of this hypothesis were consistent with past research from different industries (Babakus et al., 1996; Piercy et al., 1999) that examined the relationship between satisfaction with sales territory design and sales force behavioral performance.

Hypothesis Seven

$H7_a$ suggested that satisfaction with sales territory design is positively correlated to the level of sales force outcome performance. This hypothesis was strongly supported by the significant positive correlation between these two measures. The result of this hypothesis was consistent with prior research conducted by Babakus et al. (1996) and Piercy et al. (1999) from different industries that found a strong relationship between satisfaction with sales territory design and sales force outcome performance.

Structural Equation Model

Although correlations from the present study provide support for the majority of the hypotheses developed, a more complete test of the hypothesized relationships was the structural equation model. According to Goldberger (1973) when the observed variables contain measurement errors and the interesting relationship is among the latent variables employing structural equation models is more useful than regression models. To control for differential measurement errors in the estimation of latent variable parameters, a structural equation model (SEM) was developed and tested.

Kline (2005) provides general guidelines for the absolute magnitudes of path coefficients within structural equation models. The guidelines are based on recommendations by Cohen about effect size interpretations of correlations (as cited in Kline, 2005, p. 122). According to Cohen, standard path coefficients with absolute values less than .10 indicate a "small" effect. Standard path coefficients with values around .30 indicate a "typical" or "medium" effect. Standard path coefficients with values ≥ .50 indicate a "large" effect. According to Kline (2005), these guidelines should not be rigidly interpreted. For example, one standardized path coefficient of .49 and another .51 should not be considered as qualitatively different because the former indicates a "medium" effect and the latter a "large" effect (Kline, 2005)

The results from the structural equation model suggested that sales force outcome performance has the greatest influence and a "large" effect on sales organization effectiveness in sales organizations within the pharmaceutical industry. Sales force behavioral performance has the greatest influence and a "large" effect on sales force outcome performance. This finding is consistent with past research by Piercy et al. (1999) and Babakus et al. (1996) with respect to other industries. Sales territory design also has an influence on sales organization effectiveness, mainly through its significant relationship with sales force behavioral performance. Based on the guidelines provided by Cohen (as cited in Kline, 2005, p. 122) the standard path coefficients indicate that sales territory design has a "small" effect on sales organization effectiveness and a "large" effect on sales force behavioral performance. The next largest influence on sales organization effectiveness is from the indirect effect of sales force behavioral performance. The standard path coefficient indicates that sales force behavioral performance has a "medium" indirect effect on sales organization effectiveness. The direct relationship between sales force behavioral performance and sales force outcome performance and the indirect relationship with sales organization effectiveness through sales force outcome performance are both positive and significant.

In contrast to the findings from past research (Piercy et al., 1999) in different industries, behavior-based sales management control was not strongly related to the degree of satisfaction with sales territory design. In addition, contrary to the findings from Piercy et al. in other industries, sales territory design did not have the largest overall effect on sales organization effectiveness. Finally, the results from the present study demonstrated a non-significant positive correlation between satisfaction with sales territory design and the levels of sales force outcome performance. This differs from past research by Piercy et al. that found no direct correlation between satisfaction with sales territory design and the level of sales force outcome performance in different industries. The standardized parameter estimates from the model are shown in Figure 4.

Most of the model relationships are as predicted: sales territory design related directly to sales organization effectiveness, but only affected sales force behavioral performance significantly; sales force outcome performance influence sales organization effectiveness directly and was strongly associated with levels of sales force behavioral performance. The sales management control system was related positively and significantly to sales force behavioral performance, and to a lesser degree, to sales force outcome performance and to the level of satisfaction with sales territory design. The remainder of this chapter will discuss the implications and recommendations from the study findings.

147

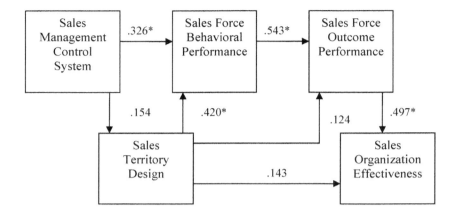

Figure 4. Model of sales organization effectiveness with standardized parameter

estimates (*N* = 151).

---

* Significant at $p \leq .05$

Implications of the Findings

The findings represented by the model in Figure 4 offer strong support for past

research in other industries that suggested systems of sales management control play a

critical role in: (a) designing effective field sales organizations, and (b) influencing

behavioral and outcome performance (Babakus et al., 1996; Cravens et al., 1993; Grant &

Cravens, 1996, Piercy et al., 1999). Consistent with prior research (Babakus et al., 1996;

Cravens et al., 1993, Piercy et al., 1999) in other industries, the results from the present

study suggested that pharmaceutical district manager satisfaction with sales territory

design is directly related to sales organizational effectiveness. However, unlike prior

research (Piercy et al., 1999), the sales territory design relationship to sales organization effectiveness was the significant relationship with respect to sales force behavioral performance. This is important because sales force behavioral performance demonstrated a significant relationship to sales force outcome performance, and sales force outcome performance had a significant relationship to sales organization effectiveness. In addition, behavioral-based management control was found to have a strong relationship to sales force behavioral performance. These findings supported past sales management principles that had not been tested empirically in sales organizations within the pharmaceutical industry.

The strong relationship found between sales force behavioral performance and outcome performance contributed to the research about sales management control. The results strongly suggested that pharmaceutical district managers expect salespeople to perform well on both behavior and outcome performance measures. These results extend and build on the findings of Babakus et al. (1996), Cravens et al. (1993) and Piercy et al. (1999) in other industries that suggested a significant positive relationship between behavior and outcome performance. Consistent with past research by Babakus et al. and Piercy et al., the results from the present study contradicted the relationship proposed by Anderson and Oliver (1987). Anderson and Oliver predicted that salespeople operating under behavior-based control systems would perform poorly on outcome measures of performance. This finding is important because Anderson and Oliver conducted seminal research on systems of behavioral and outcome sales management control.

The findings from the present study highlighted the critical role of the district manager in influencing sales force performance and effectiveness in sales organizations within the pharmaceutical industry. A key implication is that relevant sales force behavioral activities such as technical knowledge, sales planning, and sales presentations when properly performed should lead to outcome performance. Results from the present study suggested that sales force outcome performance had the greatest influence on sales organization effectiveness. This finding can help pharmaceutical district managers understand the relationships between sales management control, sales territory design, sales force performance, and sales organization effectiveness. Prior to the present study, limited empirical research existed about the relationships of the sales management control constructs within pharmaceutical sales organizations.

Contrary to the findings by Piercy et al. (1999) from other industries, the results of the structural equation model tested did not find significant correlations between sales territory design and sales organization effectiveness. Instead, sales territory design demonstrated a direct influence on sales organizational effectiveness, mainly through its significant relationship with sales force behavioral performance. The results suggested that pharmaceutical sales representatives perform better and their effectiveness is greater when they are satisfied with sales territory design because of its significant relationship with sales force behavioral performance, which leads to sales organization effectiveness through its significant relationship to sales force outcome performance. Sales force outcome performance was found to have the greatest influence on sales organization effectiveness. These results pointed to the importance of field sales management taking a proactive role in designing territories that facilitate salespeople performing well because sales force satisfaction with sales territory design is strongly associated with sales force behavioral performance, which according to the findings, is a critical step on the path to sales organization effectiveness in sales organizations within the pharmaceutical industry.

Implications for Pharmaceutical Sales Force Leadership

The results of the present study provide leaders of pharmaceutical sales organizations with empirical support for the basic sales-management principles that were supported only by observation or personal experience previously. The results suggested that the path to sales organization effectiveness in pharmaceutical sales organizations starts with improving sales force behavioral performance. This was supported by the findings, thus indicating that sales force behavioral performance has the greatest influence on outcome performance and that outcome performance has the greatest influence on sales organization effectiveness. This is contrary to prior research conducted by Piercy et al. (1999) in other industries, which found the greatest influence on sales organization effectiveness was sales territory design. As a result, sales leaders within sales organizations in the pharmaceutical industry need to invest time and resources in improving district managers' abilities to increase sales force behavioral performance.

The results of the present study suggested that the primary path to improving sales force behavioral performance in the pharmaceutical industry is ensuring sales force satisfaction with sales territory design. The results suggested that sales leaders in the pharmaceutical industry will need to actively involve pharmaceutical district managers in decisions to change sales force territory assignments, selling effort distributions across field units, and other actions leading to improved satisfaction with sales territory design. The findings suggested that improving sales force satisfaction with sales territory design leads to improved sales force behavioral performance, which according to the results, leads to sales organization effectiveness through its significant correlation to sales force outcome performance.

The next level of influence on sales force behavioral performance is behavior-based sales management control. These results pointed to the importance of pharmaceutical district managers focusing a disproportionate amount of time and effort on monitoring, directing, evaluating, and rewarding salespeople. The results of the present study suggested that the combination of satisfaction with sales territory design and sales force behavioral performance was the foundation of sales force outcome performance, which leads to sales organization effectiveness. This finding supported the need for sales leadership in the pharmaceutical industry to employ behavioral-based systems of sales management control in their sales organizations.

Finally, these findings have important implications for the approach of leaders within pharmaceutical sales organizations with respect to investment in district manager selection and training. Based on the findings, leaders within pharmaceutical sales organizations should select district manager candidates who demonstrate skills and competencies in the design of sales territory and behavioral-based management control approaches. In addition, district manager training should include sales territory design and sales management control. According to Goldsmith and Goldsmith (2004), many sales organizations evaluate the wrong competencies when selecting sales managers. The primary sales managers' hiring criteria for many sales organizations is previous individual sales performance. According to Goldsmith and Goldsmith, past individual sales performance is not the best predictor of sales managers' effectiveness.

Based on the findings from the present study improving sales force behavioral performance is indirectly related to increased sales organization effectiveness because of the significant relationship to sales force outcome performance. Therefore, sales leaders

152

in the pharmaceutical industry should invest time and resources to improve sales force behavior performance. The findings suggested that sales force behavioral performance can be improved by effective sales territory design and influencing sales force behavior and outcome performance through behavioral-based sales management control. As a result, sales leaders should develop current and future district managers' skills in both sales territory design and behavior-based sales management approaches.

Recommendation for Action by Stakeholders

Expenditures for the compensation and management of pharmaceutical sales forces account for a substantial portion of many pharmaceutical companies' annual operating budgets. According to Seget (2004), pharmaceutical companies' return on investment has decreased due to increased sales force promotional expenses and lower revenue growth. Increased competition, healthcare cost containment measures, and increased promotional expenses mandate the need for stakeholders, executives, and employees to understand the drivers of sales force performance in pharmaceutical sales organizations and the development of appropriate and effective sales management control initiatives. Based on the results of the present study, the best predictor of sales organization effectiveness, outcome performance, is strongly related to sales force behavioral performance.

The strong relationship found between sales force behavioral performance and outcome performance highlighted a critically important sales management issue: managers expect salespeople to perform well on both dimensions of performance. Managers see a positive link between behavior and results. A key implication is that relevant sales force behavior activities when performed well should lead to favorable

153

outcome performance. As a result, stakeholders in the pharmaceutical industry must closely measure and monitor sales force behavioral performance.

The results of the present study suggested that the path to sales force behavioral performance is directly related to sales territory design and sales management control. Based on these findings, stakeholders should invest a disproportionate amount of time and resources in both areas. The results strongly suggested that the greater the extent of behavioral-based management control and satisfaction with sales territory design, the greater the sales force behavioral performance, which leads to greater outcome performance and sales organization effectiveness.

Recommendations for Future Research

The findings from the present study provided important information for pharmaceutical sales leaders about factors that may increase sales organization effectiveness. However, the research was limited to the variables and sample studied. The remainder of this section provides recommendations for future research.

First, the results of the present research suggested that a need exists to better understand the relative influence of sales manager monitoring, directing, evaluating, and rewarding in the context of an overall sales management control system and its influence on sales force behavioral performance. It was noted that in the present study the district manager activity of directing showed a weaker relationship with sales force behavioral performance than was the case for the other elements of behavior-based sales management control. It would be valuable to understand these interrelationships as a basis for designing effective systems of sales management control in pharmaceutical sales organizations. In other words, while the present study concurs with Babakus et al.

(1996) and Piercy et al. (1999) in so much that it showed the more behavior-based control activities are pursued, the better the sales force behavioral performance, it would be useful to understand more thoroughly the mix of such activities that leads to higher sales force behavioral performance in pharmaceutical sales organizations. While it is often suggested that sales manager coaching activities are important, linking different degrees and types of coaching to outcomes would be of immense value to district managers.

Second, the present study confirms earlier findings from other industries that sales territory design influences sales force behavioral and outcome performance, and hence sales organization effectiveness. Clearly, while sales territory design has been demonstrated to have an influence on performance, the design of sales territory is not normally a factor within the control of the individual salesperson and, to some extent, is not under the control of the district manager. As a result, consistent with Piercy et al.'s (1999) recommendation, a key question is the extent to which ineffective or outdated sales territory designs represent an uncontrollable factor that should be assessed in salesperson performance evaluations. By bringing attention to the important role played by sales territory design on the sales management process, these studies suggest that future evaluations of sales force performance and sales organization effectiveness should include explicit consideration of the role and influence of sales territory design factors.

Third, the results suggested that behavioral-based sales management control was not related to satisfaction with sales territory design. Based on the results of the present study, sales territory design has a significant influence on behavioral performance and behavioral performance on outcome performance and requires further investigation. It may be useful to understand the relationships between these two constructs within pharmaceutical sales organizations more thoroughly, especially because, unlike previous research findings (Piercy et al, 1999) from other industries, this study found that sales territory design and behavioral-based sales management control is strongly related to sales force behavioral performance.

Fourth, the findings from this research indicated that sales territory design had a positive non-significant correlation with sales force outcome performance. This finding was contrary to prior research examining the same relationships (Piercy et al, 1999) in other industries. Because this study found outcome performance has a significant and direct relationship to sales organization effectiveness, it may be beneficial to understand this relationship within pharmaceutical sales organizations. The cost of employing a field sales force is expensive in the pharmaceutical industry. As a result, leaders in sales organizations in the pharmaceutical industry need to identify ways to influence outcome performance through choices about sales territory design.

Fifth, value may exist for examining the behavioral-based sales management control and sales territory design constructs from the perspective of the individual salesperson rather than the district manager. It would be useful to understand the influence of behavioral-based control and sales territory design issues with the greatest influence on pharmaceutical sales representatives motivation and behavior, and hence sales representatives' effectiveness. Some evidence exists that in less effective sales organizations, district manager performance is low due to high sales representative turnover (Aggarwal, Tanner, & Castleberry, 2004). High representative turnover has been attributed to the quality of salesperson-sales manager relationships, rewards and recognition, and role ambiguity (Aggarwal et al., 2004) and dissatisfaction with sales territory design (Cravens et al., 2003). As a result, understanding the relationship between sales territory design and behavior-based sales management control from the individual salesperson's perspective may provide insight to sales leaders in pharmaceutical sales organizations about ways to increase sales organization effectiveness.

Last, the measurement of study constructs was based on district manager assessment of their own activities and those of their field sales unit. As a result, findings from the present study reflect district manager perceptions of their field sales unit. According to Baldauf et al. (2001), when using self-reported information some upward bias might be inherent in such data. While past and present research evaluating systems of sales management control demonstrated adequate reliability and validity, more comprehensive measures could be developed and tested that increase construct validity in future studies.

Summary

This quantitative study made use of an explanatory correlation research design to examine the relationships between sales management control, sales territory design, sales force performance, and sales organization effectiveness in sales organizations within the pharmaceutical industry. The objective of the study was to explain the magnitude of the relationships of the independent variables, namely, sales management control, sales territory design, and sales force performance on the dependent variable, namely, sales organization effectiveness. The theoretical framework for the study was based on a sales management control system. According to Anderson and Oliver (1987), a control system is an organization's set of procedures for manager supervision, guidance, assessment, and compensation of its employees.

The results of the structural equation model for the present study suggested that outcome performance was a better measure of sales organization effectiveness than sales territory design. This was contrary to findings from past research in other industries (Piercy et al., 1999). The best predicator of outcome performance was behavioral performance followed by sales territory design. This finding was consistent with past research in other industries (Babakus et al., 1996; Piercy et al., 1999). In comparison, sales territory design was the best predicator of behavioral performance, followed by sales management control. This finding was consistent with past research in other industries (Babakus et al., 1996; Piercy et al., 1999).

The model in the present study tested the influence of the system of sales management control on sales force behavioral performance and outcome performance and the influence of sales territory design on sales force behavioral performance. Contrary to past research findings from different industries (Babakus et al., 1996; Piercy et al., 1999), the findings from the present study indicate that sales management control did not have a significant relationship with sales territory design. In addition, contrary to the findings by Piercy et al. (1999) in other industries, sales territory design does not appear to have a large direct influence on sales organization effectiveness.

Chapter 5 concludes this research study. The findings suggested that improving sales organization effectiveness within sales organization in the pharmaceutical industry starts with sales force behavioral performance. The findings suggested that sales force behavioral performance is strongly related to sales force outcome performance. Sales force outcome performance was found to have the strongest relationship to sales organizational effectiveness. To improve sales force behavioral performance, stakeholders in the pharmaceutical industry must invest time and resources in improving sales territory design and behavioral-based management control approaches. Both sales territory design and behavioral-based management control were strongly related to sales force behavioral performance. The findings suggested that pharmaceutical sales organizations that invest disproportionately in both sales territory design and behavioral-based management control could improve their sales forces' behavioral performance, which may lead to sales force outcome performance, followed by their sales' organization effectiveness.

REFERENCES

Accenture. (2003a). *The High Performance Workforce Study 2002/2003*. Retrieved August 20, 2005, from http://www.accenture.com/Global/Changing Performance.htm.

Accenture. (2003b). *Selling in Turbulent Times Survey*. Retrieved August 20, 2005, from http://www.accenture.com./Global/Changing Performance.htm.

Achrol, R. W. (1991). Evolution of the marketing organization: New forms for turbulent environments. *Journal of Marketing, 19*(7), 78-79. Retrieved October 10, 2005, from ProQuest database.

Aggarwal, P., Tanner, J., & Castleberry, S. (2004). Factors affecting propensity to leave: A Study of salespeople. *Marketing Management Journal, 14(1)*, 90-102. Retrieved June 10, 2007, from ProQuest database.

Allen, E. K. (2001). An examination of the integration of learning modalities and personality types into sales message delivery by a select group of national pharmaceutical sales representatives during sales presentations to physicians. (Doctoral dissertation, Wilmington College, 2001). *Dissertation Abstracts International, 32*, 145-151.

Anderson, E. (1985). The salesperson as outside agent or employee: A transaction cost analysis. *Marketing Science, 4*(5), 234-254. Retrieved October 10, 2005, from ProQuest database.

Anderson, E., & Oliver, R. L. (1987). Perspectives on behavior-based versus outcome-based sales force control systems. *Journal of Marketing, 51*(10), 76-88. Retrieved October 10, 2005, from ProQuest database.

Anderson, J. C., & Gerbing, D. W. (1988). Structural equation modeling in practice: A review and recommended two-step approach. *Psychological Bulletin, 103*(3), 411-423. Retrieved October 10, 2005, from ProQuest database.

Arbuckle, J. L. (2005). AMOS *6.0 Users Guide*. Chicago: SPSS, Inc.

Avila, R. A, Fern, E. F., & Mann, K. (1988). Unraveling Criteria for Assessing the Performance of Salespeople: A Causal Analysis. *Journal of Personal Selling & Sales Management, 3*(6), 45-54.

Babakus, E., Cravens, D. W., Grant, K., Ingram, T. N., & LaForge, R. W. (1996). Investigating the relationships among sales management control, sales territory design, salesperson performance, and sales organization effectiveness. *International Journal of Research in Marketing, 13*(4), 345-63. Retrieved October 10, 2005, from ProQuest database.

Baldauf, A., Cravens, D. W., & Piercy, N. F. (2000). Examining business strategy, sales management, and salesperson antecedents of sales organization effectiveness. *Journal of Personal Selling & Sales Management, 18*(5), 474-508. Retrieved October 10, 2005, from ProQuest database.

Baldauf, A., Cravens, D. W., & Piercy, N. F. (2001). Examining the consequences of sales management control strategies in European field sales organizations. *International Marketing Review, 18*(5), 474-508. Retrieved October 10, 2005, from ProQuest database.

Baldauf, A., Cravens, D. W., & Piercy, N. F. (2005). Sales management control, research-synthesis and agenda for future research. *Journal of Personal Selling and Sales Management, 1*(9), 7-26. Retrieved October 10, 2005, from ProQuest database.

Barker, E. H., & Jennings, K. M. (1999). Dysfunctional organization control mechanisms: An example. *Journal of Applied Management Studies*, *8*(2), 20-26. Retrieved October 10, 2005, from ProQuest database.

Basu, A. K., Srinvason, R. L., & Staelin, R. (1985). Sales force compensation plans: An agency theoretic perspective. *Marketing Science*, *4*(12), 267-291. Retrieved October 10, 2005, from ProQuest database.

Behrman, D. N., & Perreault, W. D. (1982). Measuring the performance of industrial salespersons. *Journal of Business Research*, *10*(4), 335-370. Retrieved October 10, 2005, from ProQuest database.

Behrman, D. N., & Perreault, W. D. (1984). A role stress model of the performance and satisfaction of industrial salespeople. *Journal of Marketing*, *48*(7), 9-21. Retrieved October 10, 2005, from ProQuest database.

Bentler, P. M., & Chou, C. P. (1987). Practical issues in structural modeling. *Sociological Methods and Research*. 16(1): 78-117. Retrieved June 1, 2007, from ProQuest database.

Bergen, M., Dutta, S., & Walker, O. C. (1992). Agency Relationships in Marketing: A Review of the Implications and Applications of Agency and Related Theories. *Journal of Marketing, 56*(3), 1-24. Retrieved October 10, 2005, from ProQuest database.

Beswick, C. A., & Cravens, D. W. (1977). A multistage decision model for sales force management. *Journal of Marketing Research, 14*(5), 134-144. Retrieved October 10, 2005, from ProQuest database.

Blessington, M., & O'Connell, W. (1995). *Sales reengineering from the outside in.* New York: McGraw-Hill.

Bohrnstedt, G. W. (1983). *Handbook of survey research.* New York: Academic Press.

Browne, M. W., & Cudeck, R. (1993). Single sample cross-validation indices for covariance structures. *Multivariate Behavioral Research, 24,* 445-455.

Bureau of Labor Statistics (1997). Employment by Major Occupational Group, 1986, 1996 and Projected 2006. Retrieved October 15, 2005, from http://www.stats.bls.gov/emptab6.htm.

Bush, R. P., Bush, A. J., Ortinau, D. J., & Hair, J. F. (1990). Developing a behavior-based scale to assess retail salesperson performance. *Journal of Retailing, 66*(8), 119-136. Retrieved October 10, 2005, from ProQuest database.

Byrne, B. N. (2001). *Structural Equation Modeling with AMOS.* Rahway, NJ: Lawrence Erlbaum Associates.

Challagalla, G. N., & Shervani, T. (1996). Dimensions and types of supervisory control: Effects on salesperson performance and satisfaction. *Journal of Marketing, 60*(9), 89-105. Retrieved October 10, 2005, from ProQuest database.

Churchill, G. A., Ford, N. M., Hartley, S.W., & Walker, O.C. (1985). The determinants of salesperson performance: A meta-analysis. *Journal of Marketing Research, 22*(8), 103-118. Retrieved October 10, 2005, from ProQuest database.

Churchill, G. A., Ford, N. M., & Walker, O. C. (1997). *Sales force management* (5th ed.) Homewood, IL: Irwin.

Cohen, L., & Manion, L. (1994). *Research methods in education* (4th ed.). London: Routledge.

Comer, L. B., Jolson, M. A., Dubinsky, A. J., & Yammarino, F. Y. (1995). When the sales manager is a woman: An exploration into the relationship between salespeople's gender and their responses to leadership styles. *Journal of Personal Selling and Sales Management, 15*(4), 17-33. Retrieved October 10, 2005, from ProQuest database.

Cooke, E. F. (1999). Control and motivation in sales management through the compensation plan. *Journal of Marketing Theory and Practice, 18*(10), 80-83. Retrieved October 10, 2005, from ProQuest database.

Corcoran, K. J., Peterson, L. K., Baitch, D. B. & Barrett, M. F. (1996). *High performance sales organizations*. Chicago: Irwin Professional.

Cornell, W. B. (1928). *Industrial organization and management*. New York: Ronald.

Cortada, J. W. (1993). *TQM for sales and marketing management.* New York: McGraw-Hill.

Cravens, D. W., Ingram, T. N., LaForge, R. W., & Young, C. E. (1993). Behavior-based and outcome-based sales force control systems. *Journal of Marketing, 57*(7), 47-59. Retrieved October 10, 2005, from ProQuest database.

Cravens, D. W., Woodruff, R. B., & Stamper, J. C. (1972). An analytical approach for evaluating sales territory performance. *Journal of Marketing, 36*(4), 31-37. Retrieved October 10, 2005, from ProQuest database.

Creswell, J. W. (2002). *Education research: Planning, conducting, and evaluating quantitative and qualitative research*. New Jersey: Upper Saddle River.

Cron, W. L., & Levey, M. (1987). Sales management performance evaluations: A residual income perspective. *Journal of Personal Selling and Sales Management*, 10(9), 57-66. Retrieved October 10, 2005, from ProQuest database.

Cronbach, L. (1970). *Essentials of psychological testing* (3rd ed.). New York: Harper and Row.

Curry, D., & Frost, J. (2001). On the right path: Sales careers in pharma. *Pharmaceutical Executive, 34*(8), 15-18, Retrieved October 10, 2005, from ProQuest database.

Darmon, R. Y. (1993). Where do the best sales force profit producers come from? *Journal of Personal Selling & Sales Management, 13*(6), 17-29. Retrieved October 10, 2005, from ProQuest database.

Davis, R. (1934). The capabilities of market-driven organizations. *Journal of Marketing, 58*(3), 37-52. Retrieved October 10, 2005, from ProQuest database.

Day, G. S. (1997). Aligning the organization to the market. In D. R. Lehmann & K. E. Jocz (Eds.), *Reflections on the futures of marketing* (pp. 67-93). Retrieved October 10, 2005, from ProQuest database.

Deci, E. L. (1975). *Intrinsic motivation*. New York: Plenum Press.

Dickson, P. R. (1994). *Marketing management*. Texas: Dryden Press.

Dubinsky, A. J., & Barry, T. E. (1982). A survey of sales management practices. *Industrial Marketing Management, 11*(9), 133-141. Retrieved October 10, 2005, from ProQuest database.

Dubinsky, A. J., Yammarino, F. J., Jolson, M. A. & Spangler, W. D. (1995).

    Transformational leadership: An initial investigation in sales management.

    Journal of Personal Selling & Sales Management, 15(3), 17-28. Retrieved

    October 10, 2005, from ProQuest database.

Dutton, H. P. (1925). *Business organization and management*. Chicago: A. W. Shaw.

Eisenhardt, K. M. (1985). Control: Organizational and economic approaches.

    Management Science, 31(4), 134-149. Retrieved October 10, 2005, from

    ProQuest database.

Fan, X., Thompson, B., & Wang, L. (1999). Effects of sample size, estimation method,

    and model specification on structural equation modeling fit indexes. *Structural*

    Equation Modeling (6): 56-83.

Flamholtz, E. G., Das, T. K., & Tsui, A. S. (1985). Toward an integrative framework of

    organizational control. *Accounting, Organizations and Society, 10*(1), 35-50.

    Retrieved October 10, 2005, from ProQuest database.

Fornell, C., & Larcker, D.F. (1981). Evaluating structural equation models with

    unobservable variables and measurement error. *Journal of Marketing Research,*

    18, 39-50.

Fraenkel, J. R., & Wallen, N. E. (2000). *How to design and evaluate research in*

    education (4th ed.). Boston: McGraw-Hill.

Futrell, J. E., Swan, J. E., & Todd, J. T. (1976). Job performance related to management

    control systems for pharmaceutical salesman. *Journal of Marketing Research,*

    22(6), 25-33. Retrieved October 10, 2005, from ProQuest database.

Ganesan, S., Weitz, B. A., & John, G. (1993). Hiring and promotion policies in

    sales force management: Some antecedents and consequences. *Journal of*

    Personal Selling & Sales Management, 13(1), 15-26. Retrieved October 10, 2005,

    from ProQuest database.

Giacobbe, R. W. (1991). Adaptive selling behavior and sales performance

    effectiveness: A contingency approach (Doctoral dissertation, Arizona State

    University, 1991). *Dissertation Abstracts International, 64,* 401.

Giglioni, G. B., & Bedian, A. G. (1974). A conspectus of management control theory:

    1900-1972. *Academy of Management Journal, 17*(9), 292-305. Retrieved October

    15, 2005, from ProQuest database.

Goldberger, A. S. (1973). Structural equation models: An overview. In A. S.

    Goldberger And O.D. Duncan (Eds.): *Structural equation models in the social*

    sciences. New York: Seminar Press.

Goldsmith, D. A., & Goldsmith, L. A. (2004). Eight essentials to build an effective sales

    manager. *Business Journal, 18*(15), 15-19. Retrieved June 10, 2007, from

    ProQuest database.

Grant, K., & Cravens, D. W. (1996). Examining sales force performance in

    organizations that use behavior-based sales management processes. *Industrial*

    Marketing Management, 25(4), 361-371. Retrieved October 15, 2005, from

    ProQuest database.

Hatcher, L. (1994). A *step-by-step approach to using SAS for factor analysis and*

    structural equation modeling. Cary, NC: SAS Institute Inc.

Heide, C. P. (1999). *Dartnell's 30th sales force compensation survey.*
Chicago: Dartnell.

Hun, L., & Bentler, P. M. (1999). Cut-off Criteria for Fit Indexes in Covariance
Structure Analysis: Conventional criteria versus new alternatives. *Structural
Equation Modeling*, 6, 1-55.

Jackson, D. W., Keith, J. E., & Schlacter, J. L. (1983). Evaluation of selling
performance: A study of current practices. *Journal of Personal Selling & Sales
Management, 33*(4), 42-51. Retrieved October 15, 2005, from ProQuest.
database.

Jaworski, B. J. (1988). Toward a theory of marketing control: Environmental context,
control types, and consequences. *Journal of Marketing, 52*(7), 23-39. Retrieved
October 10, 2005, from ProQuest database.

Jaworski, B. J., & Kohli, A. K. (1991). Supervisory feedback: Alternative types and
their impact on salespeople's performance and satisfaction. *Journal of Marketing
Research, 13*(5), 190-200. Retrieved October 10, 2005, from ProQuest database.

John, G., & Weitz, B. (1989). Sales force compensation: An empirical investigation of
factors related to the use of salary versus incentive compensation. *Journal of
Marketing Research, 26*(9), 1-14. Retrieved October 10, 2005, from ProQuest
database.

Jöreskog, K.G., & Sörbom, D. (2006). *LISREL 8.80.* Chicago: Scientific Software
International.

Kalton, G., & Kasprzyk, D. (1982). *Imputing for missing survey responses.* Paper
presented at the 1982 Proceedings of the Section on Survey Research.

Kline, R. B. (1998). *Principles and practice of structural equation modeling*. New York: Guilford Press.

Kline, R. B. (2005). *Principles and practice of structural equation modeling* (2nd ed.). New York: Guilford Press.

Krafft, M. (1999). An Empirical Investigation of the Antecedents of Sales Force Control Systems. *Journal of Marketing, 63*(2), 120-134. Retrieved October 10, 2005, from ProQuest database.

LaForge, R. W. (1992). *Sales management—analysis and decision making* (2nd ed.) Fort Worth, TX: Dryden Press.

LaForge, R. W., & Cravens, D. W. (1985). Empirical and judgment-based sales force decision models: A comparative analysis. *Decision Sciences, 16*(3), 177-195. Retrieved October 10, 2005, from ProQuest database.

Lagace, R. R., & Howe, V. (1988). *Salesperson performance: An evaluation of the Behrman and Perreault scale, efficiency and effectiveness in marketing*. Chicago: American Marketing Association.

Lal, R., & Staelin, R. S. (1986). Sales force compensation plans in environments with asymmetries information. *Marketing Science, 5*(2), 179-198. Retrieved October 10, 2005, from ProQuest database.

Lamont, L. M., & Lundstrom, W. J. (1974). Defining industrial sales behavior: A factor analytic study. *American Marketing Association, 68*(7), 493-498. Retrieved October 10, 2005, from ProQuest database.

Lawler, E. E. (1973). *Motivation in work organizations*. Monterey, CA: Books/Cole.

Lawler, E. E. (1976). *In Handbook of industrial and organization psychology*. Chicago: Rand McNally.

Leigh, T. W., & McGraw, P. F. (1989). Mapping the procedural knowledge of industrial sales personnel: A script-theoretic investigation. *Journal of Marketing, 53*(11), 16-30. Retrieved October 10, 2005, from ProQuest database.

Lichtner, W. O. (1924). *Planned control in manufacturing*. New York: Ronald.

Little, R. J. A., & Rubin, D. B. (2002). *Statistical analysis with missing data* (2nd Ed.). New York: Wiley.

Lodish, L. M. (1980). Vaguely right sales force allocation decisions. *Harvard Business Review, 52*(3), 119-124. Retrieved October 15, 2005, from ProQuest database.

Lopez, T. B. (2000). Examining the impact of control systems on the implementation of market-oriented and customer-oriented strategies. (Doctoral dissertation, Louisiana Tech University, 2000). *Dissertation Abstracts International, 61,* 1924.

Lucas, A. (1996). Leading edge—down and out: Corporate layoffs tighten the belts of company sales forces. *Sales and Marketing Management, 22*(4), 80-83. Retrieved October 10, 2005, from ProQuest database.

MacCallum, R .C., Browne, M. W., & Sugwara, H. M. (1996). Power Analysis and Determination of Sample Size for Covariance Structure Modeling. *Psychological Methods*, 1, 130-149.

MacKinzie, S. B., Podkasoff, P. M., & Fetter, R. (1993). The impact of organizational citizenship behavior on evaluation of salesperson performance. *Journal of Marketing, 19*(5), 70-80. Retrieved October 10, 2005, from ProQuest database.

Mallin, M. L. (2005). A framework of control and trust in sales governance. (Doctoral

 dissertation, Kent State University, 2005). *Dissertation Abstracts International,*

 66, 2648.

Moncrief, W. C. (1986). Selling activity and sales position taxonomies for industrial

 sales forces. *Journal of Marketing Research, 23*(2), 261-270. Retrieved October

 10, 2005, from ProQuest database.

Moore, J. R., Eckrich, D. W., & Carlson, L. T. (1986). A hierarchy of industrial selling

 competencies. *Journal of Marketing Education, 8*(6), 79-88. Retrieved October

 10, 2005, from ProQuest database.

Morris, M. H., Davis, D. L., Allen, J. W., Avila, R. A., & Chapman, J. (1991). Assessing

 the relationships between performance measures, managerial practices, and

 satisfaction when evaluating the sales force. *Journal of Personal Selling & Sales

 Management, 24*(5), 25-35. Retrieved October 10, 2005, from ProQuest database.

Mount, M. K., & Barrick, M. R. (1995). The big five personality dimensions:

 Implications for research and practice in human resources management. *Research

 in Personnel and Human Resources Management, 13*(3), 153-200. Retrieved

 October 10, 2005, from ProQuest database.

Muczyk, J. P., & Gable, M. (1987). Managing Sales Performance Through a

 Comprehensive Performance Appraisal System. *Journal of Personal Selling and

 Sales Management*, 7(1), 41-42. Retrieved October 10, 2005, from University of

 Phoenix Website: http://www.proquest.

Nunnally, J. C. (1978). *Psychometric theory* (2nd ed.). New York: McGraw-Hill.

Nunnally, J. C., & Bernstein, I. H. (1994). *Psychometric theory*. New York: McGraw-
Hill, Inc.

Oliver, R. L., & Anderson, E. (1994). An empirical test of the consequences of
behavior-and outcome-based control systems. *Journal of Marketing, 58*(7), 53-57.
Retrieved October 10, 2005, from ProQuest database.

Oliver, R. L., & Anderson, E (1995). Behavior and outcome-based sales control
systems: Evidence and consequences of pure-form and hybrid governance.
Journal of Personal Selling & Sales Management, 15(4), 1-15. Retrieved October
10, 2005, from ProQuest database.

Onyemah, V. I. (2003). Sensitivity of salesperson's performance to incongruity in control
systems: A varying parameter model. (Doctoral dissertation, Institute European
d'Administration des Affaires, 2003). *Dissertation Abstracts International, 64*,
2573.

Oschrin, E. (1918). Vocational tests for retail saleswoman. *Journal of Applied
Psychology, 2*(6), 148-155. Retrieved October 15, 2005, from ProQuest database.

Ouchi, W. G. (1977). The relationship between organizational structure and
organizational control. *Administrative Science Quarterly, 22*(3), 95-112.
Retrieved October 10, 2005, from ProQuest database.

Ouchi, W. G. (1979). A conceptual framework for the design of organizational control
mechanisms. *Management Science*, *25*(9), 833-848. Retrieved October 10, 2005,
from ProQuest database.

Ouchi, W. G., & Maguire, M. A. (1975). Organizational control: Two functions. *Administrative Science Quarterly, 20*(9), 559-569. Retrieved October 10, 2005, from ProQuest database.

Pasold, P. W. (1975). The effectiveness of various modes of sales behavior in different markets. *Journal of Marketing Research, 12*(6), 171-176. Retrieved October 10, 2005, from ProQuest database.

Peters, C. L., & Enders, C. (2002). A primer for the estimation of structural equation models in the presence of missing data. *Journal of Targeting, Measurement and Analysis for Marketing, 11*, 81-95.

Piercy, N. F. (1985). *Marketing organization: An analysis of information processing, power and politics*. London: Unwin Hyman.

Piercy, N. F., Cravens, D. W., & Lane, N. (2001). Sales Manager Behavior Control and Its Consequences: The Impact of Gender Differences. *Journal of Personal Selling & Sales Management, 21*(1), 39-49. Retrieved October 10, 2005, from ProQuest database.

Piercy, N. F., Cravens, D. W., & Lane, N. (2003). Sales manager behavior control strategy and its consequences: The impact of manager gender differences. *Journal of Personal Selling & Sales Management, 23*(3), 221-237. Retrieved October 10, 2005, from ProQuest database.

Piercy, N. F., Cravens, D. W., & Morgan, N. A. (1998). Sales performance and behavior-based management processes in business-to-business sales organizations. *European Journal of Marketing, 32*(1), 79-100. Retrieved October 10, 2005, from ProQuest database.

Piercy, N. F., Cravens, D. W., & Morgan, N. A. (1999). Relationships between sales

 management control, territory design, sales force performance and sales

 organization effectiveness. *British Journal of Management, 10*(5), 95-111.

 Retrieved October 10, 2005, from ProQuest database.

Piercy, N. F., Low, G. S., & Cravens, D. W. (2004). Examining the effectiveness of

 sales management control practices in developing countries. *Journal of World*

 Business, 39(3), 255-267. Retrieved October 10, 2005, from ProQuest database.

Plank, R. E., & Dempsey, W. A. (1980). A Framework for personal selling to

 organizations. *Industrial Marketing Management, 14(8)*, 243-249. Retrieved

 October 10, 2005, from ProQuest database.

Plank, R. E., & Reid, D. A. (1994). The mediating role of sales behaviors: An alternative

 perspective of sales performance and effectiveness. *Journal of Personal Selling &*

 Sales Management, 3(4), 45-49. Retrieved October 10, 2005, from ProQuest

 database.

Pushkala, R., Wittmann, C. M., & Rauseo, N. A. (2006). Leveraging CRM For Sales:

 The Role Organizational Capabilities in Successful CRM Implementation.

 Journal of Personal Selling & Sales Management, 26(1), 39-53. Retrieved

 October 10, 2005, from ProQuest database.

Ramaswami, S. N. (2002). Influence of control systems on opportunistic behaviors of

 salespeople: A test of gender differences. *Journal of Personal Selling & Sales*

 Management, 22(3), 172-188. Retrieved October 10, 2005, from ProQuest

 database.

Rangaswamy, A., Sinha, P., & Zoltners, A. A. (1990). An integrated model-based approach for sales force structuring. *Marketing Science, 9*(4), 279-298. Retrieved October 10, 2005, from ProQuest database.

Reeves, T. K., & Woodward, J. (1970). *The study of managerial control in industrial organizations: Behavior and control.* London: Oxford University Press.

Ryans, A. B., & Weinberg, C. B. (1979). Territory sales response. *Journal of Marketing Research, 16*(6), 453-465. Retrieved October 10, 2005, from ProQuest database.

Ryans, A. B., & Weinberg, C. B. (1987). Territory sales response models: Stability over time. *Journal of Marketing Research, 24*(8), 229-233. Retrieved October 10, 2005, from ProQuest database.

Ryerson, A. T. (2003). Behavioral aspects of self-efficacy: A measurement of sales performance. (Doctoral dissertation, Nova Southeastern University, 2003). *Dissertation Abstracts International, 64*, 4019.

Saenz, C. (2004). Factors influencing prescribing in the pharmaceutical industry: Patient and physician intent. (Doctoral dissertation, Nova Southeastern University, 2004). *Dissertation Abstracts International, 65*, 3476.

Sahoo, A. (2005). Drug safety in the post-Vioxx era: New legislation, regulation and company strategies in Europe and the U.S. *Business Insights Ltd, 8*(3), 24-45. Retrieved October 10, 2005, from ProQuest database.

Seget, S. (2004). Pharmaceutical sales force strategies: Driving ROI through best practice in targeting, management, outsourcing and technology. *Business Insights Ltd, 9*(6), 78-98. Retrieved October 10, 2005, from ProQuest database.

Skelton, N. (2004). Sales force effectiveness: The new strategic imperative. *European Pharmaceutical Executive, 10*(3), 101-104. Retrieved October 10, 2005, from ProQuest database.

Slater, S., & Olson, E. M. (2000). Strategy Type and Performance: The Influence of Sales Force Management. *Strategic Management Journal, 21*(8), 813-829. Retrieved October 10, 2005, from ProQuest database.

Smith, G. A., Ritter, D., & Tuggle, W. P. (1995). The fundamental questions. *Marketing Management, 33*(6), 43-48. Retrieved October 10, 2005, from ProQuest database.

Spiro, R. L., & Weitz, B. A. (1990). Adaptive selling: Conceptualization, measurement, and nomological validity. *Journal of Marketing Research, 27*(5), 61-69. Retrieved October 10, 2005, from ProQuest database.

Stanton, W. J., & Buskirk, R. H. (1983). *Management of the Sales Force*. Homewood, IL: Richard D. Irwin Inc.

Stathakopoulos, V. (1996). Sales force control: A synthesis of three theories. *Journal of Personal Selling & Sales Management, 21*(2), 98-105. Retrieved October 15, 2005, from ProQuest database.

Steiger, J. H. (1990). Structural Model Evaluation and Modifications: An interval estimation approach. *Multivariate Behavioral Research*, 25, 173-180.

Sujan, H., Sujan, M., & Bettman, J. R. (1988). Knowledge structure differences between more effective and less effective salespeople. *Journal of Marketing Research*, 23(2), 41-49. Retrieved October 15, 2005, from ProQuest database.

Swanson, A. M. (2003). A theory and taxonomy of individual sales performance. (Doctoral dissertation, University of Minnesota, 2003). *Dissertation Abstracts International, 54*, 5827

Szymanski, D. M. (1988). Determinants of selling effectiveness: The importance of declarative knowledge to the personal selling concept. *Journal of Marketing, 52*(3), 64-77. Retrieved October 15, 2005, from ProQuest database.

Tabachnick, B. G., & Fidell, L. S. (2001). *Using multivariate statistics* (4th Ed.). New York: Allyn and Bacon.

Tannenbaum, A. S. (1968). *Control in organizations.* New York: McGraw-Hill.

Thompson, J. B. (2002). A conjoint analysis of selection criteria used in the screening phase of pharmaceutical sales. (Doctoral dissertation, The University of Mississippi, 2002). *Dissertation Abstracts International, 63*, 4575.

Vinchur, A. J., Schippmann, J. S., Switzer, F. S., & Roth, P.L. (1998). A meta-analytic review of the predictors of job performance for salespeople. *Journal of Applied Psychology, 83*(4), 586-597. Retrieved October 15, 2005, from ProQuest database.

Walker, O. C., Churchill, G. A., & Ford, N. M. (1977). Motivation and performance in industrial selling: Present knowledge and needed research. *Journal of Marketing Research, 14*(6), 156-168. Retrieved October 10, 2005, from ProQuest database.

Walker, O. C., Churchill, G. A., & Ford, N. M. (1979). Selected conceptual and empirical issues concerning the motivation and performance of the industrial sales force. *Journal of Marketing Research, 12*(8), 126-138. Retrieved October 10, 2005, from ProQuest database

Weber, M. (1947). *The theory of social and economic organization.* New York: The
   Free Press.

Webster, F. E. (1992). The changing role of marketing in the corporation. *Journal of
   Marketing, 56*(6), 1-17. Retrieved October 10, 2005, from ProQuest database.

Weitz, B. A. (1978). The relationship between salesperson performance and
   understanding of customer decision making. *Journal of Marketing Research,
   15*(8), 501-516. Retrieved October 10, 2005, from ProQuest database.

Weitz, B. A. (1979). A critical review of personal selling research: The need for
   contingency approaches. *Journal of Marketing Research, 10*(9), 76-126.
   Retrieved October 10, 2005, from ProQuest database.

Weitz, B. A. (1981). Effectiveness in sales interactions: A contingency framework.
   Journal of Marketing, 45(3), 85-103. Retrieved October 10, 2005, from ProQuest
   database.

Weitz, B. A., Sujan, H., & Sujan, M. (1986). Knowledge, motivation, and adaptive
   behavior: A framework for improving selling effectiveness. *Journal of Marketing,
   50*(2), 174-191. Retrieved October 10, 2005, from ProQuest database.

Wilkins, A. L., & Ouchi, W. G. (1983). Efficient cultures: Exploring the relationship
   between culture and organizational performance. *Administrative Science
   Quarterly, 28*(1), 468-481. Retrieved October 10, 2005, from ProQuest database.

Williamson, O. E. (1981). The economics of organization: The transaction cost
   approach. *American Journal of Sociology, 87*(3), 548-577. Retrieved October 10,
   2005, from ProQuest database.

Williamson, O. E. (1985). *The economic institutions of capitalism.* New York: The Free Press.

Woodard, J. (1970). *Industrial organizations: Behavior and control.* London: Oxford University Press.

Zhong, X. Y. (2001). The relationship between selling ability and sales performance. (Doctoral dissertation, Purdue University, 2001). *Dissertation Abstracts International, 63,* 281.

Zoltners, A. A., & Lorimer, S. E. (2000). Sales territory alignment: An overlooked productivity tool. *Journal of Personal Selling & Sales Management, 20*(3), 115-121. Retrieved October 15, 2005, from ProQuest database.

Zoltners, A. A., & Sinha, P. (1983). Sales territory alignment: A review and model. *Management Science, 29*(7), 1237-1256. Retrieved October 15, 2005, from ProQuest database.

Zoltners, A. A., Sinha, P., & Zoltners, G. A. (2001). *A complete guide to accelerating sales force performance.* New York: Amacom.

Dear _____:

Sales management at Octagon Pharmaceutical is interested in your opinions regarding factors of sales force performance. We would like you to take part in a brief survey. The aggregate results of this survey will be used to improve sales force management practices within Octagon Pharmaceutical. Your participation will provide valuable feedback and help to develop sales management training initiatives and tools to better meet your needs.

The sponsor of the study, Octagon Pharmaceutical, has agreed to allow this research to be conducted by Eric Longino. Eric is currently a group product director within operating company A and is currently pursuing a Doctor of Business Administration degree from the University of Phoenix. He will be conducting this research as part of his dissertation on pharmaceutical sales force effectiveness. All study participants name and survey responses will be held in strict confidence and only aggregated data will be reported to sales leadership at Octagon Pharmaceutical.

We seek your support in helping to better understand what factors impact pharmaceutical sales force performance. The information you provide will be a tremendous help in this effort.

Our survey will take approximately 45 minutes to complete. All study participants will receive an executive summary of study findings.

Timing of this survey is important. Please complete the survey within 14 days of receipt.

Eric Longino
Operating Company A

APPENDIX B: INFORMED CONSENT

Date:

Dear_____:

I am currently a doctoral candidate at the University of Phoenix, pursuing a Doctor of Business Administration degree. I am currently employed with operating company A, which is a pharmaceutical operating company within the Octagon Pharmaceutical. The purpose of this letter is to request your participation in a quantitative correlation research study, which will entail district managers from operating companies within Octagon Pharmaceutical completing a survey. Completion of the survey is expected to take no longer than 45 minutes.

The purpose of the study is to increase sales management understanding of the factors that improve pharmaceutical sales force performance. Understanding the factors that improve pharmaceutical sales force performance could help sales managers within Octagon Pharmaceutical improve sales force performance. Your participation could provide sales leadership at Octagon Pharmaceutical valuable insights regarding the predictors of sales force performance. The name of study participants and all survey responses will be kept strictly confidential. Study participants will receive an executive summary of the results.

In this research, there are no foreseeable risks to you except by chance your survey responses are not kept confidential. To ensure confidentiality all data will be coded using a numerical prefix that is known only to the researcher. List of codes will be maintained in a locked cabinet and accessible only to the researcher. All data will be secured in a locked cabinet accessible only by the researcher for a period of three years. All data will then be destroyed so as to not be accessible nor reconstructed.

You must be 18 years or older to participate in this study. Your participation in this study is voluntary. If you choose not to participate or to withdraw from the study at any time, you can do so without penalty or loss of benefit to yourself. Only senior sales leadership at participating Octagon Pharmaceutical operating companies and the three members of my dissertation committee and me will review the study results.

By signing this form you are acknowledging that you understand the nature of the study, the potential risks to you as a participant and the means by which your identity will be kept confidential. Your signature also indicates that you are 18 years or older and that you give your permission to voluntarily serve as a participant in the study described.

_____   _____
Participant Signature   Date

Please return the signed consent form to my attention at the address above within 10 days of receipt. If you have any questions concerning the study, please contact me or reply to this correspondence via my electronic email address. Thank you in advance for your participation.

Sincerely Yours,

Eric Longino

APPENDIX C: RESEARCH QUESTIONNAIRE

Scale Items

Scale	**Items**	**Source**

Behavior-Based Sales Management Control

To what extent do you:

Monitor
1. Spend time with salespeople in the field.   Based on Cravens et al. (1993)
2. Make joint calls with salespeople.
3. Regularly review call reports from salespeople.
4. Monitor the day-to-day activities of salespeople.
5. Observe the performance of salespeople in the field.
6. Pay attention to the extent to which salespeople travel.
7. Closely watch salespeople's expense accounts.
8. Pay attention to the credit terms that salespeople quote customers.

Direct
1. Encourage salespeople to increase their sales results by rewarding them for their achievements
2. Actively participate in training of salespeople on the job.
3. Regularly spend time coaching salespeople.
4. Discuss performance evaluations with salespeople.
5. Help salespeople develop their potential

Evaluate
1. Evaluate the number of sales calls made by salespeople.
2. Evaluate the profit contribution achieved by each salesperson.
3. Evaluate the sales results of each salesperson.
4. Evaluate the quality of sales presentations made by salespeople.
5. Evaluate the professional development of salespeople.

Reward
1. Provide performance feedback to salespeople on a regular basis.
2. Compensate salespeople based on the quality of their sales activities.
3. Use incentive compensation judgments based on the sales results achieved by salespeople.
4. Make incentive compensation judgments based on the sales results achieved by salespeople.
5. Reward salespeople based on their sales results.

6. Use non-financial incentives to reward salespeople for their achievements.
7. Compensate salespeople based on the quantity of their sales activities.

Satisfaction with Sales Territory Design

My level of satisfaction with:

1. The number of accounts in my territories.

Based on Babakus et al. (1996)

2. The number of large accounts in my territories.
3. The sales productivity in my territories.
4. The geographical size of my territories.
5. The number of calls made in my territories.
6. The amount of travel required in my territories.
7. The market potential in my territories.
8. The number of territories in my sales unit.
9. The assignment of salespeople to my territories.
10. The equivalence in workload across territories
11. The overall design of my territories.

Sales force Performance

How well are the salespeople in your unit performing:

Outcome Performance

1. Producing a high market share for your company.

Based on Behrman and Perreault (1982) and Cravens et al. (1993)

2. Making sales of those products with the highest profit margins.
3. Generating a high level of dollar sales.
4. Quickly generating sales of new company products/services.
5. Identifying and selling to major accounts.
6. Producing sales or blanket contracts with long-term profitability.
7. Exceeding all sales targets and objectives during the year.

184

Technical Knowledge	1.	Knowing the design and specifications of company products/services.	
	2.	Knowing the application and functions of company products/services.	
	3.	Keeping abreast of your company's production and technological developments.	
Adaptive Selling	1.	Experimenting with different sales approaches.	Based on Spiro and Weitz (1990)
	2.	Being flexible in the selling approaches used.	
	3.	Adapting selling approaches from one customer to another.	
	4.	Varying sales styles from situation to situation.	
Teamwork	1.	Generating considerable sales volume from team sales (sales jointly by two or more salespeople).	John and Weitz JMR (1989), p. 13
	2.	Building strong working relationships with other people in our company.	
	3.	Working very closely with non-sales employees to close sales.	
	4.	Coordinating very closely with other company. employees to handle post-sales problems and service.	
	5.	Discussing selling strategies with people from various departments.	
Sales Presen- tation	1.	Listening attentively to identify and understand the real concerns of customers.	Based on Behrman and Perreault (1982) and Cravens et al. (1993)
	2.	Convincing customers that they understand their unique problems and concerns.	
	3.	Using established contacts to develop new customers.	
	4.	Communicating their sales presentation clearly and concisely.	
	5.	Working out solutions to a customer's questions and objections.	
Sales Planning	1.	Planning each sales call.	Based on Babakus et al. (1996)
	2.	Planning sales strategies for each customer.	
	3.	Planning coverage of assigned territory/customer	

responsibility.

| | 4. | Planning daily activities. | |

Sales Support
1. Providing after sales service.

2. Checking on product delivery.
3. Handling customer complaints.
4. Follow up on product use.
5. Troubleshooting application problems.
6. Analyzing product use experience to identify new product/service ideas.

Sales Organization Effectiveness

Sales and market share effect-tiveness
1. Sales volume compared to your major competitor (past 24 months).   Cravens et al. (1993)

2. Market share compared to your major competitor.
3. Sales volume compared to sales unit objectives.
4. Market share compared to sales unit objectives.

Profita-bility
1. Profitability compared to your major competitor.

2. Profitability compared to sales unit objectives.

Customer Satisfact-ion
1. Customer satisfaction compared to your major competitors.

2. Customer satisfaction compared to sales unit objectives.

APPENDIX D: BOXPLOTS

Monitor

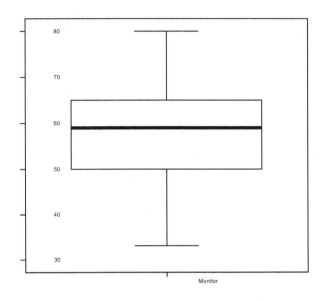

Direct

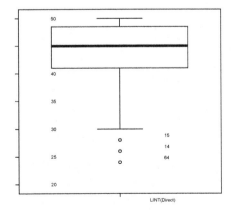

Evaluate

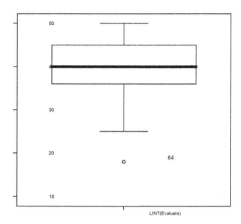

Reward

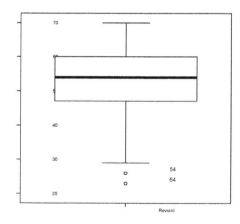

Design

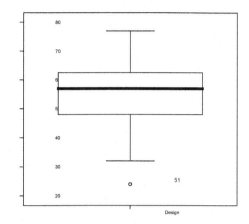

Outcome Performance

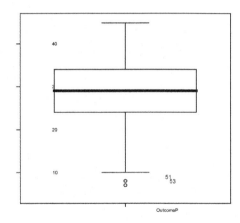

Tech

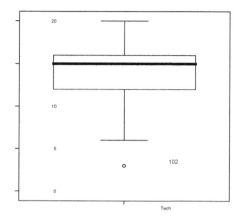

Adaptive

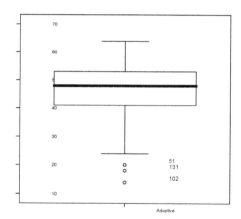

Teamwork

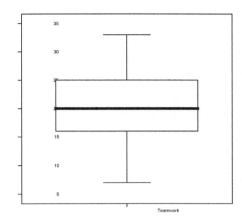

Presentation

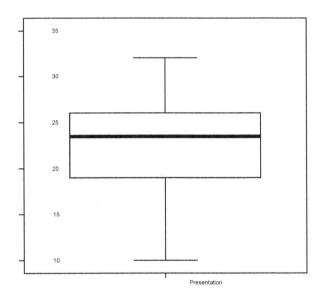

Planning

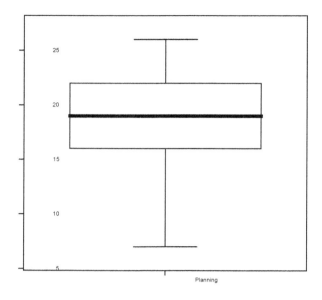

Support

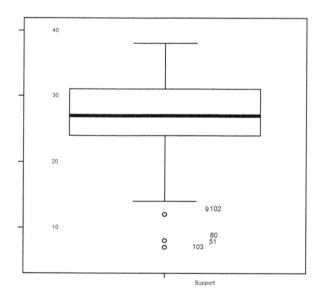

Effective

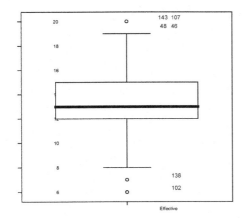

Profit

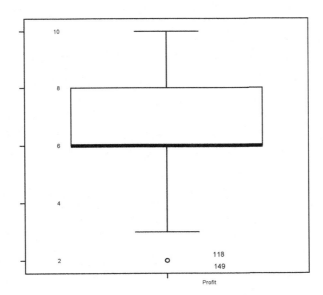

Satisfaction

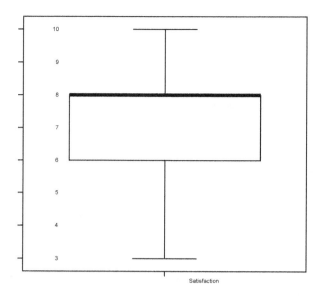

APPENDIX E: MODIFICATION INDICES

Covariance: Group number 1—Default model

		Modification indices	Parameter change
es3 -->	CONTROL	5.728	9.587
e12 -->	res2	5.634	.728
e8 -->	CONTROL	4.488	7.902
e7 -->	CONTROL	5.442	8.824
e7 -->	res3	13.639	13.486
e7 -->	te8	8.962	10.178
e6 -->	CONTROL	5.537	5.103
e6 -->	res3	6.122	5.180
e6 -->	te9	4.436	1.446
	te12	5.003	-1.035

		Modification indices	Parameter change
e6 -->			
e6 -->	te7	17.282	8.218
e5 -->	CONTROL	4.204	4.391
e5 -->	res3	15.535	8.149
e5 -->	te8	11.814	6.617
e5 -->	te7	21.334	9.017
e5 -->	te6	30.471	6.179
e4 -->	CONTROL	5.023	6.426
e4 -->	res3	9.510	8.536
e4 -->	te8	7.601	7.106
e4 -->	te7	32.635	14.931

		Modification indices	Parameter change
e4 -->	te5	22.035	6.947
e3 -->	res3	4.193	-4.000
e3 -->	te7	9.214	-5.560
e2 -->	te6	16.105	-1.605
e2 -->	te5	22.006	-1.853
e2 -->	te3	7.422	.812
rr4 -->	res3	13.293	14.910
rr4 -->	te8	11.388	12.849
rr4 -->	te7	4.192	7.906
rr4 -->	te4	5.814	7.058

Regression weights: Group number 1—Default model

			Modification indices	Parameter change
OUTPERF	<---	CONTROL	5.728	.243
Profit	<---	BEHPERF	4.942	-.107
Profit	<---	Adaptive	4.872	-.031
Profit	<---	Tech	5.839	-.104
Satisfaction	<---	BEHPERF	7.074	.123
Satisfaction	<---	Adaptive	6.964	.036
Satisfaction	<---	Tech	9.591	.128
OutcomeP	<---	CONTROL	4.488	.200
OutcomeP	<---	Support	7.685	.203
OutcomeP	<---	Present	7.417	.300
OutcomeP	<---	Teamwork	5.754	.216
OutcomeP	<---	Reward	11.913	.200
Support	<---	CONTROL	5.442	.223
Support	<---	OUTPERF	12.394	.288
Support	<---	EFFECT	7.633	1.743
Support	<---	Effective	5.212	.417
Support	<---	OutcomeP	12.561	.247
Support	<---	Planning	13.166	.452
Support	<---	Present	12.601	.396

			Modification indices	Parameter change
Support	<---	Teamwork	23.317	.441
Support	<---	Monitor	4.560	.112
Support	<---	Reward	7.494	.161
Planning	<---	CONTROL	5.537	.129
Planning	<---	OUTPERF	6.979	.124
Planning	<---	EFFECT	5.539	.851
Planning	<---	Effective	6.430	.265
Planning	<---	OutcomeP	6.738	.104
Planning	<---	Support	14.254	.161
Planning	<---	Present	17.997	.271
Planning	<---	Reward	6.640	.087
Present	<---	CONTROL	4.204	.111
Present	<---	OUTPERF	15.044	.179
Present	<---	EFFECT	7.135	.954
Present	<---	Effective	4.794	.226
Present	<---	OutcomeP	15.441	.155
Present	<---	Support	17.596	.176
Present	<---	Planning	23.214	.340
Present	<---	Teamwork	15.743	.205
Present	<---	Monitor	4.619	.064

			Modification indices	Parameter change
Present	<---	Reward	6.152	.083
Teamwork	<---	CONTROL	5.023	.163
Teamwork	<---	OUTPERF	7.297	.167
Teamwork	<---	OutcomeP	7.850	.148
Teamwork	<---	Support	26.916	.292
Teamwork	<---	Present	13.015	.305
Teamwork	<---	Monitor	4.814	.087
Teamwork	<---	Reward	8.485	.130
Adaptive	<---	OUTPERF	4.341	-.092
Adaptive	<---	OutcomeP	4.388	-.079
Adaptive	<---	Support	7.803	-.112
Tech	<---	Planning	12.271	-.088
Tech	<---	Present	13.001	-.081
Tech	<---	Reward	5.002	-.027
Reward	<---	OUTPERF	11.130	.305
Reward	<---	OutcomeP	11.936	.270
Reward	<---	Support	4.293	.172
Reward	<--	Teamwork	5.333	.236

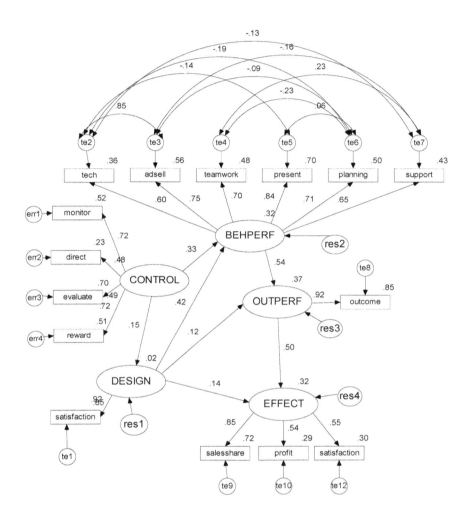

APPENDIX G: AMOS FINAL OUTPUT

Notes for Group (Group number 1)
The model is recursive.
Sample size = 151

Parameter summary (Group number 1)

	Weights	Covariances	Variances	Means	Intercepts	Total
Fixed	24	0	2	0	0	26
Labeled	0	0	0	0	0	0
Unlabeled	17	9	18	0	0	44
Total	41	9	20	0	0	70

Notes for Model (Default model)

Computation of degrees of freedom (Default model)

Number of distinct sample moments: 120
Number of distinct parameters to be estimated: 44
Degrees of freedom (120 - 44): 76

Result (Default model)
Minimum was achieved
Chi-square = 86.188
Degrees of freedom = 76
Probability level = .199

Estimates (Group number 1 - Default model)
Scalar Estimates (Group number 1 - Default model)
Maximum Likelihood Estimates
Regression Weights: (Group number 1 - Default model)

202

			Estimate	S.E.	C.R.	P	Label
SALESDESIGN	<---	CONTROL	.223	.147	1.521	.128	
BEHPERF	<---	SALESDESIGN	.081	.019	4.204	***	
BEHPERF	<---	CONTROL	.091	.028	3.205	.001	
OUTPERF	<---	SALESDESIGN	.093	.072	1.291	.197	
OUTPERF	<---	BEHPERF	2.103	.456	4.614	***	
EFFECT	<---	SALESDESIGN	.014	.010	1.403	.161	
EFFECT	<---	OUTPERF	.067	.017	3.911	***	
Direct	<---	CONTROL	.463	.093	4.972	***	
Monitor	<---	CONTROL	1.132	.164	6.896	***	
Tech	<---	BEHPERF	1.000				
Adaptive	<---	BEHPERF	3.788	.285	13.274	***	
Teamwork	<---	BEHPERF	2.232	.360	6.203	***	
Present	<---	BEHPERF	2.202	.348	6.325	***	
Planning	<---	BEHPERF	1.666	.305	5.459	***	
Support	<---	BEHPERF	2.585	.453	5.711	***	
OutcomeP	<---	OUTPERF	1.000				
Satisfaction	<---	EFFECT	1.000				
Profit	<---	EFFECT	1.033	.213	4.850	***	
Effective	<---	EFFECT	2.608	.503	5.188	***	
Design	<---	SALESDESIGN	1.000				
Evaluate	<---	CONTROL	.699	.103	6.808	***	
Reward	<---	CONTROL	1.000				

Standardized Regression Weights: (Group number 1 - Default model)

Estimate

			Estimate
SALESDESIGN	<---	CONTROL	.154
BEHPERF	<---	SALESDESIGN	.420
BEHPERF	<---	CONTROL	.326
OUTPERF	<---	SALESDESIGN	.124
OUTPERF	<---	BEHPERF	.543
EFFECT	<---	SALESDESIGN	.143
EFFECT	<---	OUTPERF	.497
Direct	<---	CONTROL	.478
Monitor	<---	CONTROL	.724
Tech	<---	BEHPERF	.603
Adaptive	<---	BEHPERF	.746
Teamwork	<---	BEHPERF	.695
Present	<---	BEHPERF	.837
Planning	<---	BEHPERF	.708
Support	<---	BEHPERF	.655
OutcomeP	<---	OUTPERF	.921
Satisfaction	<---	EFFECT	.546
Profit	<---	EFFECT	.541
Effective	<---	EFFECT	.849
Design	<---	SALESDESIGN	.921
Evaluate	<---	CONTROL	.703
Reward	<---	CONTROL	.717

Covariances: (Group number 1 - Default model)

			Estimate	S.E.	C.R.	P	Label
te5	<-->	te6	.439	1.310	.335	.737	
te4	<-->	te7	5.294	2.558	2.069	.039	
te3	<-->	te7	-5.301	3.348	-1.583	.113	
te3	<-->	te6	-1.710	2.407	-.711	.477	
te2	<-->	te7	-1.722	1.273	-1.352	.176	
te2	<-->	te6	-1.376	.839	-1.640	.101	
te2	<-->	te5	-.898	.435	-2.064	.039	
te2	<-->	te3	12.462	2.111	5.904	***	
te4	<-->	te6	-2.911	1.311	-2.220	.026	

Correlations: (Group number 1 - Default model)

			Estimate
te5	<-->	te6	.056
te4	<-->	te7	.235
te3	<-->	te7	-.160
te3	<-->	te6	-.093
te2	<-->	te7	-.133
te2	<-->	te6	-.191
te2	<-->	te5	-.144
te2	<-->	te3	.851
te4	<-->	te6	-.232

Variances: (Group number 1 - Default model)

	Estimate	S.E.	C.R.	P	Label
CONTROL	41.756	9.517	4.388	***	
res1	86.295	11.849	7.283	***	
res2	2.211	.650	3.401	***	
res3	30.661	4.808	6.378	***	
res4	.607	.198	3.071	.002	
te8	8.719				
te1	15.716				
err4	39.535	6.644	5.951	***	
err3	20.806	3.382	6.151	***	
err2	30.364	3.827	7.935	***	
err1	48.671	8.335	5.839	***	
te2	5.735	.833	6.887	***	
te3	37.409	5.831	6.415	***	
te4	17.446	2.481	7.033	***	
te5	6.767	1.401	4.829	***	
te6	9.037	1.719	5.256	***	
te7	29.157	4.162	7.005	***	
te12	2.108	.285	7.405	***	
te10	2.299	.309	7.440	***	
te9	2.362	.933	2.531	.011	

Squared Multiple Correlations: (Group number 1 - Default model)

	Estimate
SALESDESIGN	.024
BEHPERF	.325
OUTPERF	.374

	Estimate
EFFECT	.321
Design	.849
Effective	.720
Profit	.293
Satisfaction	.298
OutcomeP	.849
Support	.429
Planning	.501
Present	.701
Teamwork	.483
Adaptive	.557
Tech	.363
Monitor	.524
Direct	.228
Evaluate	.495
Reward	.514

Matrices (Group number 1 - Default model)
Total Effects (Group number 1 - Default model)

	CONTROL	SALESDESIGN	BEHPERF	OUTPERF	EFFECT
SALESDESIGN	.223	.000	.000	.000	.000
BEHPERF	.109	.081	.000	.000	.000
OUTPERF	.251	.263	2.103	.000	.000
EFFECT	.020	.032	.141	.067	.000
Design	.223	1.000	.000	.000	.000
Effective	.052	.083	.368	.175	2.608
Profit	.021	.033	.146	.069	1.033

	CONTROL	SALESDESIGN	BEHPERF	OUTPERF	EFFECT
Satisfaction	.020	.032	.141	.067	1.000
OutcomeP	.251	.263	2.103	1.000	.000
Support	.283	.209	2.585	.000	.000
Planning	.182	.135	1.666	.000	.000
Present	.241	.178	2.202	.000	.000
Teamwork	.244	.180	2.232	.000	.000
Adaptive	.414	.306	3.788	.000	.000
Tech	.109	.081	1.000	.000	.000
Monitor	1.132	.000	.000	.000	.000
Direct	.463	.000	.000	.000	.000
Evaluate	.699	.000	.000	.000	.000
Reward	1.000	.000	.000	.000	.000

Standardized Total Effects (Group number 1 - Default model)

	CONTROL	SALESDESIGN	BEHPERF	OUTPERF	EFFECT
SALESDESIGN	.154	.000	.000	.000	.000
BEHPERF	.391	.420	.000	.000	.000
OUTPERF	.231	.353	.543	.000	.000
EFFECT	.137	.318	.270	.497	.000
Design	.141	.921	.000	.000	.000
Effective	.116	.270	.229	2	.849	.000
Profit	.074	.172	.146	269	.541
Satisfaction	.075	.174	147 271	.546	.000
OutcomeP	.213	.325	. .921	.000
Support	.256	.275	501 655	.000	.000

	CONTROL	SALESDESIGN	BEHPERF	OUTPERF	EFFECT
Planning	.277	.297	.708	.000	
Present	.327	.351	.837	.000	
Teamwork	.271	.292	.695	.000	
Adaptive	.291	.313	.746	.000	
Tech	.235	.253	.603	.000	
Monitor	.724	.000	.000	.000	
Direct	.478	.000	.000	.000	
Evaluate	.703	.000	.000	.000	
Reward	.717	.000	.000	.000	

Direct Effects (Group number 1 - Default model)

	CONTROL	SALESDESIGN	BEHPERF	OUTPERF	EFFECT
SALESDESIGN	.223	.000	.000	.000	.000
BEHPERF	.091	.081	.000	.000	.000
OUTPERF	.000	.093	2.103	.000	.000
EFFECT	.000	.014	.000	.067	.000
Design	.000	1.000	.000	.000	.000
Effective	.000	.000	.000	.000	2.608
Profit	.000	.000	.000	.000	1.033
Satisfaction	.000	.000	.000	.000	1.000

	CONTROL	SALESDESIGN	BEHPERF	OUTPERF	EFFECT
OutcomeP	.000	.000	.000	1.000	.000
Support	.000	.000	2.585	.000	.000
Planning	.000	.000	1.666	.000	.000
Present	.000	.000	2.202	.000	.000
Teamwork	.000	.000	2.232	.000	.000
Adaptive	.000	.000	3.788	.000	.000
Tech	.000	.000	1.000	.000	.000
Monitor	1.132	.000	.000	.000	.000
Direct	.463	.000	.000	.000	.000
Evaluate	.699	.000	.000	.000	.000
Reward	1.000	.000	.000	.000	.000

Standardized Direct Effects (Group number 1 - Default model)

	CONTROL	SALESDESIGN	BEHPERF	OUTPERF	EFFECT
SALESDESIGN	.154	.000	.000	.000	.000
BEHPERF	.326	.420	.000	.000	.000
OUTPERF	.000	.124	.543	.000	.000
EFFECT	.000	.143	.000	.497	.000
Design	.000	.921	.000	.000	.000
Effective	.000	.000	.000	.000	.849
Profit	.000	.000	.000	.000	.541
Satisfaction	.000	.000	.000	.000	.546
OutcomeP	.000	.000	.000	.921	.000
Support	.000	.000	.655	.000	.000
Planning	.000	.000	.708	.000	.000
Present	.000	.000	.837	.000	.000
Teamwork	.000	.000	.695	.000	.000

	CONTROL	SALESDESIGN	BEHPERF	OUTPERF	EFFECT
Adaptive	.000	.000	.746	.000	.000
Tech	.000	.000	.603	.000	.000
Monitor	.724	.000	.000	.000	.000
Direct	.478	.000	.000	.000	.000
Evaluate	.703	.000	.000	.000	.000
Reward	.717	.000	.000	.000	.000

Indirect Effects (Group number 1 - Default model)

	CONTROL	SALESDESIGN	BEHPERF	OUTPERF	EFFECT
SALESDESIGN	.000	.000	.000	.000	.000
BEHPERF	.018	.000	.000	.000	.000
OUTPERF	.251	.170	.000	.000	.000
EFFECT	.020	.018	.141	.000	.000
Design	.223	.000	.000	.000	.000
Effective	.052	.083	.368	.175	.000
Profit	.021	.033	.146	.069	.000
Satisfaction	.020	.032	.141	.067	.000
OutcomeP	.251	.263	2.103	.000	.000
Support	.283	.209	.000	.000	.000
Planning	.182	.135	.000	.000	.000
Present	.241	.178	.000	.000	.000
Teamwork	.244	.180	.000	.000	.000
Adaptive	.414	.306	.000	.000	.000
Tech	.109	.081	.000	.000	.000
Monitor	.000	.000	.000	.000	.000
Direct	.000	.000	.000	.000	.000
Evaluate	.000	.000	.000	.000	.000

	CONTROL	SALESDESIGN	BEHPERF	OUTPERF	EFFECT
Reward	.000	.000	.000	.000	.000

Standardized Indirect Effects (Group number 1 - Default model)

	CONTROL	SALESDESIGN	BEHPERF	OUTPERF	EFFECT
SALESDESIGN	.000	.000	.000	.000	.000
BEHPERF	.064	.000	.000	.000	.000
OUTPERF	.231	.228	.000	.000	.000
EFFECT	.137	.175	.270	.000	.000
Design	.141	.000	.000	.000	.000
Effective	.116	.270	.229	.422	.000
Profit	.074	.172	.146	.269	.000
Satisfaction	.075	.174	.147	.271	.000
OutcomeP	.213	.325	.501	.000	.000
Support	.256	.275	.000	.000	.000
Planning	.277	.297	.000	.000	.000
Present	.327	.351	.000	.000	.000
Teamwork	.271	.292	.000	.000	.000
Adaptive	.291	.313	.000	.000	.000
Tech	.235	.253	.000	.000	.000
Monitor	.000	.000	.000	.000	.000
Direct	.000	.000	.000	.000	.000
Evaluate	.000	.000	.000	.000	.000
Reward	.000	.000	.000	.000	.000

Modification Indices (Group number 1 - Default model)
Covariances: (Group number 1 - Default model)

M.I.	Par Change
4.922	-.869

	M.I.	Par Change
e6 --> e12		
rr4 --> es3	8.544	10.947
rr4 --> e12	4.092	-1.800
rr4 --> e8	7.704	9.816

Variances: (Group number 1 - Default model)

	M.I.	Par Change

Regression Weights: (Group number 1 - Default model)

			M.I.	Par Change
Profit	---	Adaptive	4.936	-.031
Profit	---	Tech	5.836	-.104
Satisfaction	---	Adaptive	6.891	.035
Satisfaction	---	Tech	9.543	.128
OutcomeP	---	Reward	5.738	.131
Reward	---	OUTPERF	8.829	.267
Reward	---	OutcomeP	9.442	.237

Model Fit Summary

CMIN

Model	NPAR	CMIN	DF	P	CMIN/DF
Default model	44	86.188	76	.199	1.134
Saturated model	120	.000	0		
Independence model	15	1009.035	105	.000	9.610

RMR, GFI

Model	RMR	GFI	AGFI	PGFI
Default model	2.310	.934	.895	.591
Saturated model	.000	1.000		
Independence model	12.556	.433	.352	.379

Baseline Comparisons

Model	NFI Delta1	RFI rho1	IFI Delta2	TLI rho2	CFI
Default model	.915	.882	.989	.984	.989
Saturated model	1.000		1.000		1.000
Independence model	.000	.000	.000	.000	.000

Parsimony-Adjusted Measures

Model	PRATIO	PNFI	PCFI
Default model	.724	.662	.716
Saturated model	.000	.000	.000
Independence model	1.000	.000	.000

NCP

Model	NCP	LO 90	HI 90

NCP

Model	NCP	LO 90	HI 90
Default model	10.188	.000	37.235
Saturated model	.000	.000	.000
Independence model	904.035	805.975	1009.539

FMIN

Model	FMIN	F0	LO 90	HI 90
Default model	.575	.068	.000	.248
Saturated model	.000	.000	.000	.000
Independence model	6.727	6.027	5.373	6.730

RMSEA

Model	RMSEA	LO 90	HI 90	PCLOSE
Default model	.030	.000	.057	.873
Independence model	.240	.226	.253	.000

AIC

Model	AIC	BCC	BIC	CAIC
Default model	174.188	184.696	306.949	350.949
Saturated model	240.000	268.657	602.074	722.074
Independence model	1039.035	1042.617	1084.294	1099.294

ECVI

Model	ECVI	LO 90	HI 90	MECVI
Default model	1.161	1.093	1.342	1.231
Saturated model	1.600	1.600	1.600	1.791
Independence model	6.927	6.273	7.630	6.951

HOELTER

Model	HO ELTER .05	HO ELTER .01
Default model	170	188
Independence model	20	22

APPENDIX H: VERBAL SCRIPT

To: District Managers within Octagon Pharmaceutical

From: National Sales Director

Date: March 26, 2007

Re: Sales Force Effectiveness Survey

Greetings! I would like to take this opportunity to share information about pharmaceutical sales management research that will be conducted among district managers within Octagon Pharmaceutical sales organizations in the month of March. In an effort to improve our sales management practices and training initiatives, we would like to capture insight from pharmaceutical sales district managers within Octagon Pharmaceutical sales organizations regarding the factors that drive pharmaceutical sales force performance. Your role in this study is vital – we need you to provide your perspective via a confidential electronic questionnaire on what factors improve sales force performance. The information we obtain from this study will be used to evolve our sales management practices and sales management training approaches.

It is important for you to know that all survey responses will be captured <u>completely anonymously</u>. Results will be encoded to insure anonymity, as our goal is not to evaluate in *any way, shape or form* a particular district manager – but to look at trends in the aggregate. Again, the intent of this initiative is to capture your perspective on what factors drive sales force performance. The results will not be attributed to any district manager in the sales force.

To accomplish this, Eric Longino of operating company A will conduct the research. He will send out via email to district managers of participating sales organizations a link that provides access to an electronic survey. The email will include an introduction to participants, letter of participation, survey link and instructions for survey completion. The survey will take approximately 45 minutes to complete.

Your participation in this study is voluntary. If you choose not to participate or to withdraw from the study at any time, you can do so without any penalty or loss of benefit to yourself.

If you have any questions, please feel free to contact me at my email address

Thanks in advance for your participation.

National Sales Director

APPENDIX I: RESEARCH HYPOTHESES

$H1_A$: There is a significant correlation between the level of sales force behavioral performance and the level of sales force outcome performance.

$H1_O$: There is no significant correlation between the level of sales force behavioral performance and the level of sales force outcome performance.

$H2_A$: There is a significant correlation between the level of salesperson outcome performance and the level of sales organization effectiveness.

$H2_O$: There is no significant correlation between the level of salesperson outcome performance and the level of sales organization effectiveness.

$H3_A$: There is a significant correlation between the extent of behavior-based sales management control and the level of salesperson behavioral performance.

$H3_O$: There is no significant correlation between the extent of behavior-based sales management control and the level of salesperson behavioral performance.

$H4_A$: There is a significant correlation between the extent of behavior-based sales management control and the level of satisfaction with sales territory design.

$H4_O$: There is no significant correlation between the extent of behavior-based sales management control and the level of satisfaction with sales territory design.

$H5_A$: There is a significant correlation between the extent of satisfaction with sales territory design and the level of sales organization effectiveness.

$H5_O$: There is no significant correlation between the extent of satisfaction with sales territory design and the level of sales organization effectiveness.

$H6_A$: There is a significant correlation between the extent of satisfaction with the sales territory design and the level of sales force behavioral performance.

$H6_O$: There is no significant correlation between the extent of satisfaction with the sales territory

   design and the level of sales force behavioral performance.

$H7_A$: There is a significant correlation between the extent of satisfaction with the sales territory

   design and the level of sales force outcome performance.

$H7_O$: There is no significant correlation between the extent of satisfaction with the sales territory

   design and the level of sales force outcome performance.

APPENDIX J: PERMISSION TO USE MATERIALS

```
----Original Message-----
From: Smith, Stephanie (ELS-OXF) [mailto:ST.Smith@elsevier.com]
Sent: Friday, November 10, 2006 7:07 AM
To: Eric Longino
Subject: RE: Obtain Permission
```

We hereby grant you permission to reproduce the material detailed below in your thesis at no charge subject to the following conditions:

1.   If any part of the material to be used (for example, figures) has appeared in our publication with credit or acknowledgement to another source, permission must also be sought from that source. If such permission is not obtained then that material may not be included in your publication/copies.

2.   Suitable acknowledgment to the source must be made, either as a footnote or in a reference list at the end of your publication, as follows:

"Reprinted from Publication title, Vol number, Author(s), Title of article, Pages No., Copyright (Year), with permission from Elsevier".

3.   Reproduction of this material is confined to the purpose for which permission is hereby given.

4.   This permission is granted for non-exclusive world English rights only. For other languages please reapply separately for each one required. Permission excludes use in an electronic form. Should you have a specific electronic project in mind please reapply for permission.

5.   This includes permission for UMI to supply single copies, on demand, of the complete thesis. Should your thesis be published commercially, please reapply for permission.

Yours sincerely

Steph Smith
Rights Assistant

Elsevier Ltd
The Boulevard
Langford Lane
Kidlington
Oxford OX5 1GB

```
-----Original Message-----
From: Eric Longino
Sent: 09 November 2006 03:07
To: Rights and Permissions (ELS)
Subject: Obtain Permission
```

This Email was sent from the Elsevier Corporate Web Site and is related to Obtain Permission form:

Product: Customer Support
Component: Obtain Permission
Web server: http://www.elsevier.com
IP address: 10.10.24.149
Client: Mozilla/4.0 (compatible; MSIE 6.0; Windows NT 5.1; .NET CLR 1.0.3705)
Invoked from:
http://www.elsevier.com/wps/find/obtainpermissionform.cws_home?isSubmitt
ed=yes&navigateXmlFileName=/store/prod_webcache_act/framework_support/ob
tainpermission.xml

Request From:
Group Product Director Eric Longino
University of Phoenix
United States

Contact Details:
Telephone:
Fax:
Email Address: elongin1

To use the following material:
ISSN/ISBN:
Title: International Journal of Research in Marketing
Author(s):   Emin Babakus, David W. Cravens, Ken Grant
Volume: 13
Issue: 1
Year: 1996
Pages: 345 - 363
Article title: Invest Relationship sales management control...

How much of the requested material is to be used:
Conceptual model page 346; Table 1 page 352; Table 2 353; Table 3 and 4
page 355; Appendix A. Scale Items page 358 - 361

Are you the author: No
Author at institute: No

How/where will the requested material be used: [how_used]

Details:

I'm a doctoral student at University of Phoenix. I will be conducting a
study on sales management control within the pharmaceutical industry.
The requested material will be included in the dissertation only

Additional Info: Please confirm via email or hard copy if I can
use the requested material. I must include your confirmation in the
appendix of my dissertation proposal. I need a response ASAP. Thanks
for your consideration.

- end -

For further info regarding this automatic email, please contact:
WEB APPLICATIONS TEAM (esweb.admin@elsevier.co.uk)

CPSIA information can be obtained
at www.ICGtesting.com
Printed in the USA
BVOW09s1840011216

469514BV00006B/204/P